THE SHEARER AND THE MAGISTRATE

JOHN P. F. LYNCH

Published by John P F Lynch

Copyright © John P F Lynch 2020

Lynch, John P F
The Shearer and the Magistrate

ISBN 978-0-9923002-9-6 (pbk)
ISBN 978-0-6489446-0-7 (e-book)

 A catalogue record for this book is available from the National Library of Australia

The Author of this book accepts all responsibility for the contents and absolves any other person or persons involved in its production from any responsibility or liability where the contents are concerned. This is a work of fiction. Names, characters, businesses, places, events, locales, and incidents are either the products of the author's imagination or used in a fictitious manner. Any resemblance to actual persons, living or dead, or actual events is purely coincidental.

All rights reserved. No part of this publication may be reproduced, stored in a retrieval system, or transmitted, in any form, by any means, electronic, mechanical, photocopying, recording or otherwise, without prior permission from the author.

Typeset in Bookman Old Style 12 pt

Produced by **TB Books**
        P.O. Box 8138
        Seymour South Victoria 3660 Australia
        Email: tbbooks@collings.id.au

Cover Design by TB Books
Front Cover Picture from National Library Australia
    November by S. T. Gill 1841-43
Back Cover Picture from National Library Australia
    Early Australian Homestead by D. Cooper 1845

DEDICATION

To my Grandfather Edmund Keough (Keogh) 1866-1942 of *Woodlea Farm* – a pioneer of Tocumwal N.S.W.

DEDICATION

CONTENTS

FOREWORD vii

INTRODUCTION ix

CHAPTER ONE
    Emigrant To Immigrant 11
CHAPTER TWO
    An Unusual Welcome 43
CHAPTER THREE
    Gone Shearing 78
CHAPTER FOUR
    The Partnership 113
CHAPTER FIVE
    Testing Times 128
CHAPTER SIX
    Dreams Achieved 171

ADDENDUM
  Addendum 1 EXTRACTS FROM AN 1886 SHEARING CONTRACT 216
  Addendum 2 THE AUSTRALIAN WORKERS' UNION 218
  Addendum 3 THE SHEARERS H. Lawson ... 220
  Addendum 4 AGRICULTURE COLLEGES 222
  Addendum 5 WAGES – 1860 224

AUTHOR 226

OTHER BOOKS by J. P. F. Lynch 227

FOREWORD

As a young undergraduate in the mid 1960's I developed a love of what I would describe as social literature. This love remains today and among my favourite authors are the likes of Thomas Hardy, Charles Dickens and Jane Austen. They were the dashcams and video cameras of their day; but they were so much more than that. While the lens records images of a particular time and place in superb detail the social novelist also provides an insight into hopes and aspirations and the actual life circumstances of those living in that time and place in a way which the lens cannot do.

Australia, too, has its great chroniclers and raconteurs such as A.B. "Banjo" Paterson, Henry Lawson, C.J. Dennis, and Steele Rudd to name a few. I can still remember as a youngster lying on the lounge room floor in front of an open fire listening to a serialised version of *Dad and Dave*, based on Steele Rudd's, *On Our Selection*. I would eagerly await each new episode and remember being enthralled at the time by the seeming romance of a life on the land.

Such works are irreplaceable archival records of who we are; a snapshot of the very fabric of a society and its people in a particular time and place. Equally importantly they engage us in a way our modern media fails to do. When we are forced to engage with the words on the page and actually use our imaginations, the picture becomes so much richer for the effort.

While, *The Shearer and the Magistrate* is not derived from the lived experience of its author at the time, it is founded in a depth of historical research which gives the story a real sense of time and place. It is a relatively slim volume and, as such, rightly focuses on its central narrative, recounting the lives of two young men, of their hopes and experiences as they attempt to forge their way, in what was still, a young but rapidly growing colonial society. A chance meeting that brought them together paves the way for a series of inter-related adventures and experiences through which the reader is introduced, albeit briefly, to a rapidly growing colonial society.

The pastoral industry had developed sufficiently to require teams of shearers along the east coast to meet their needs. Melbourne had a well-established judiciary and there were clear signs of wealth and order: there was a grammar school in Geelong; and an elite, "Melbourne Club". There were also signs of society becoming more structured: country towns had their own constabularies and there were signs of local governance.

The narrative of the range of experiences detailed in this story is well crafted. It is clearly the work of someone with a genuine love of, and interest in, Australian history.

This is a simple, endearing story which leaves the reader thinking there might still be a tale or two to tell.

Kevin Dillon
B.A., Dip.ED., B.ED. M.Ed.
Cert IV (Training and Assessment)

INTRODUCTION

The colonial days of Australia brought people from all walks of life to our shore – free settlers, convicts, deserters, public servant administrators and the unscrupulous – all for different reasons. After the tumultuous early decades, the colonies gradually developed their identities. Mainly through the establishment of sheep and cattle properties and the rich farmlands. Then came the gold rush, which initially caused mayhem. Ordinary people left their employment and the farms to seek their fortune. Many shops were deserted, police left their posts and even domestic servants went to try their luck. A few found their fortune, but many came back poorer but wiser. Stability soon returned to the community.

Small towns and individuals came to the fore. Along all popular roads, about every twenty or so miles, an inn or a store was erected. They began mainly as a shanty made of canvas, saplings and bark. Some survived and became established buildings, encouraging other enterprises to join them to start a village, and hence a town.

Of the individuals, the shearers were a major workforce in the mid 1800's. They started shearing in

Queensland and worked their way south to Victoria and, after a break, headed north again for the following shearing season.

In those days, law and order was a problem, not only from the crime point of view, but also for judicial management control. The police forces had many incompetent constables while others were inadequately supervised in larger towns. Some were even ex-convicts. Justices of Peace were far and few between and there was an urgent need for magistrates in the country districts. The few magistrates that existed were mainly based in Melbourne. However, the law prevailed, the community benefited, and society remained stable and orderly.

This story is focused on two young immigrants – a coachbuilder and a lawyer, and their community contribution to the colony. One becomes a shearer/farmer and the other a magistrate/farmer. It is partly fiction, interwoven with true events. Primarily it is intended to be reminiscent of those exciting and heady colonial days.

JOHN P. F. LYNCH
OAM KSJ JP FRVAHJ

CHAPTER ONE

Emigrant To Immigrant

The River Suir tide had peaked, and the small ship was furling its last sail and was slowly losing way. Two lines had been cast from the ship, one from the bow and the other from the stern, down to two row boats. After being tied to their sterns, they were rowed to the pier. Upon reaching the pier, the lines were passed to the dock men and looped over the pier's bollards, the ship's winches were turned, pulling the ship slowly to the pier.

A customs officer and the ship owner's representative were waiting for the gangway to be placed into position. They would be the first two people to board the vessel. Once aboard they met with the captain who, after some preliminary small talk, handed over the ship's manifest and other associated documents. After satisfying himself that the ship had a clean bill of health and a brief inspection confirmed that the cargo was as declared, the customs officer left with the ship owner's representative to decide what custom import duties might be levied.

William Chadwick had been a customs officer for nearly twenty years and over the years he had risen through the ranks to be a supervisor at Waterford, a major south east Ireland seaport. He was content with life and enjoyed the freedom of his employment. He had married Jane, an innkeeper's daughter and they had a son, Alan, who had been learning coach building for four years.

After the company built a coach, young Alan Chadwick was often tasked to deliver the coach to customers throughout Ireland. Alan enjoyed his job and the outdoor life, but he had the wanderlust. As a youngster he had accompanied his father to the waterfront and gazed in awe at the sailing ships and watched the sailors climbing the rigging and tending the sails and the myriad of ropes. While delivering the coaches, he often dreamt of travelling on the high seas.

His Uncle John, his father's brother, owned a stables business serving the wealthy residents of Sydney, in the Colony of New South Wales. He always listened intently when his father read letters from him, describing what life was like in the colony. Gradually a travel plan formed – how – what – when – where. He already knew the – why. He was now twenty-four years of age and wanted to travel and see the world.

Alan wrote to his uncle without telling his father, asking him for advice on the colony and if he could get a job there. A few months later he received an answer from him offering him a job with his stables business maintaining coaches that were left in his care. He was unsure, though, if his parents would be happy with him going to the other side of the world.

Then his concern no longer mattered – Mother Nature decided. His mother suddenly became seriously ill with a chest complaint. The doctor recommended a warmer climate as the only possible chance of improvement. Ireland's damp and cold winters would be too severe for her to last more than a year or two. The doctor recommended migrating to the Australian colonies. Most educated people knew of the warmer weather in the antipodes.

His father quickly made the decision to apply to emigrate to the Colony of New South Wales. He had seen a bulletin advising that their government was seeking experienced customs officers. The rumours of gold and the effects of the Ireland potato famine still impacting Irish farmers, were both causing a dramatic increase in immigration, and in the shipping industry. Subsequently colony administrative staff had an excessive workload.

Alan was unsure what to say to his parents. Inwardly he was delighted they would all be going to Australia now, but his mother's illness upset him.

When he told his parents of his uncle's offer, they were delighted. His father had been concerned at what Alan would say when he knew that his parents were considering going to the colonies. Alan's father immediately wrote to his brother advising him that the family was coming to Sydney.

Jane's parents were, understandably, disappointed that she and her family were going to the colonies, but they realised that her health must come first. She had three sisters, so it was not as if they would be alone and without any family around them.

John Chadwick's return letter enclosed a statement from the colony's immigration agent nominating the three of them for immigration. John had paid their assisted immigration passage fee to the Colonial Treasury in Sydney. Their passage would now be free. This procedure was to encourage people of value to move to the colony, having prior employment and accommodation provided by another party on arrival. The notice from the colony waived the fees, helping to speed up the local Emigration Office requirements.

Apart from the normal family information regarding address, where and when born, where and when married and number of children, the needed information advised

– health, previous employment, wages, if pregnant, name and address of Parish Minister and whether they were on Parish relief.

The applicant was then required to sign the statement in front of two witnesses known to him or her, confirming the person to be of good character and they were considered not to be a burden to the colony by virtue of poor mental or physical health. The document also needed to be signed by a physician who had examined the person, confirming the person was free from infectious or contagious disease. Finally, a magistrate was required to certify that the signatures were authentic. Fortunately, with William's contacts through his customs duties, the paperwork was dealt with very quickly and forwarded to the Agent General.

Alan had been born in Waterford two years after his parents married. He loved his mother's delightful west coast Irish brogue. His father was from Dublin and had met his mother when she was helping her father in his inn, in which they lived. His father had only to walk several hundred yards to the customs office and Alan about a mile to the coach building yard.

Alan's uncle's stables business was also his home in Sydney town. It was a large two-story multipurpose building with stables, fodder storage and workshop on the ground floor, and a large accommodation area above, capable of accommodating William's family of three. When his father mentioned this to the emigration officer, he was advised this would ensure that the three of them would travel together as they would have accommodation provided on arrival. As they had employment offers, they would be welcomed by the Colony Agent General.

As they lived in their father-in-law's inn, they owned very little other than their clothes, some mementoes and a few heirloom pieces. They would start their new life from scratch. They hoped their decision to emigrate would mean an exciting, healthy and secure life for them. William had been formally advised that he was accepted as a Senior Customs Officer and he would be employed by the Government of the Colony of New South Wales on his arrival. Alan, as a skilled artisan, would be employed by his uncle as evidenced by his uncle's letter.

If his mother's health improved, and with her education and refined manners, it was fairly certain that, if she wished, she could obtain domestic employment. They were all optimistic that her health would recover.

The emigration process seemed to take a long time as they waited impatiently for notification of their departure date. In the meantime, many of their friends had been farewelling them with dinners and drinks.

They had lived in Waterford for many years and had a wide circle of friends. They would miss them. Although Alan had a former school friend he would be glad not to see again.

Sean Kennedy and Alan had grown up together and had been good friends. However, fate had not been kind to Sean, and he had fallen from a hay cart and broken his right leg when he was twelve years old. The accident left him with his right leg an inch shorter than his left. Even with a leather heel insert in his shoe he still limped. The viciousness of fellow students showed when they started to call him 'Limpy'. From that day on Sean had changed. He became aggressive, distrustful and withdrawn.

Alan slowly started to avoid him because of his unpleasant attitude. Other students had fights with him, and he had been suspended from school twice for his disruptive actions. His future looked grim. Alan had rarely seen him since he started work with the coach builder. Other school friends warned Alan to stay clear of him; he was trouble.

Shortly after their emigration papers had been lodged, Sean came into the inn, half drunk and spoiling for a fight.

When he saw Alan, he approached him and began sneering and shouting. 'You're too big for your boots. I'll show you all one day. Just you see, you'll remember the name Sean Kennedy.'

Alan was sitting having lunch as Sean stood over him bellowing. He tried to ignore him but eventually he stood up and told him to leave. Sean threw a wild punch at Alan but in his drunken rage fell over and ended up under a table.

Alan's grandfather watched the event unfold. He had enough of Sean's behaviour. He grabbed Sean by his collar and belt and carried him kicking and struggling out through the door to the horse trough in front of the inn and dropped him in the water. Sean did not return.

However, Sean was to be ultimately remembered throughout Ireland and England for a notorious criminal act. The week after he was ejected from the inn, he made headlines when he abused the city mayor because his council house had caught fire. He was arrested but was released when the mayor said he was sympathetic to a person who had lost his temper because his council house had burnt down, even though it appeared Sean had caused the fire by going to sleep while smoking a lighted tobacco pipe. The mayor said Sean had suffered enough. The court did not realise that Sean was in a dangerous frame of mind and was almost out of control.

The next weekend the mayor was attending the opening of the new Council Community School. Sean quietly joined the crowd and slowly jostled his way through the standing crowd to a position in front of the mayor but one row back. He quietly removed a pistol from under his coat, aimed it at the mayor's chest and fired. The ball struck the mayor in the chest and killed him instantly. Sean dropped the pistol to the ground and, during the ensuing melee, slowly crept away through the crowd.

An inquisitive young man picked up the pistol and was immediately challenged by a bystander. The crowd grabbed the man and hauled him to the nearby gaol. He was soon released from custody when he was found to be a Church of England minister and witnesses also said he was not the culprit.

Sean moved quickly to the pier. He had previously arranged to stow away on an outgoing ship with the help of a friend. The ship was long gone before he was positively identified as the assailant.

He had been recognised by a nearby member in the crowd, who was a court official during the recent court case and recognised him by his limp. The police suspected that he had escaped by sea. Several ships had sailed to different ports over the weekend – local waters, American or Australian. Which one?

William walked into the kitchen smiling from ear to ear. He had a letter in his hand. He had visited the emigration office and was presented with the response from the Agent General's office. He sat down and read the contents to Jane and Alan. They would be sailing in three weeks from Cork on the S.S. Maria. They were to travel to Cork and report to the ship owner's agent three days before departure to be further processed through the emigration system.

They were further advised, in their case, it was only a formality. It was mainly to confirm their identity and for them to be passed fit by another doctor. None of them slept deeply that night – they were travelling to the opposite side of the world – what would they find?

They wrapped their valued and fragile possessions in clothing and linen and then packed them into two trunks. They had some vases, paintings and books from Jane's grandparents and a few items of furniture – a wall hanging pendulum clock, a chest of drawers and a small carved dining room setting. William had a quality shotgun and a set of cane fishing rods.

Alan's sole items of value were his tools of trade and the illustrated book on coach building presented to him by the owner of the Coach Company of Ireland where he had completed his apprenticeship.

The customs office staff had an afternoon tea to farewell William. He was presented with a silver watch, suitably engraved, acknowledging his contribution to Her Majesty's Customs Service. The Ship Owners Agents Association gifted him with a painting of the Waterford Pier waterfront featuring the famous clock tower. After several speeches, the drinks flowed, and many stories were told of humorous events during William's career. It was a night William would not forget. It was the end of the first part of his life and now came the start of the next part.

Similarly, Alan's service was acknowledged with a small silver fob watch, engraved with his initials – A.C. For Service. Alan fitted it into his belt. The coach builders company farewell was low key compared to the Customs Office one, but it delighted Alan. He had enjoyed the working environment and the companionship of his workmates. He would miss their friendship and their cheerful workshop chatter. He was grateful that the company had given him a skilled qualification to ensure his future work potential. It was now up to him to decide if he should progress his career further or seek another.

The final farewell gathering was with both of their families, and friends, at the inn. There were about forty people. It was both a sad night and a happy night – a parting and a beginning. The evening was long but enjoyable. After many hugs, handshakes and kisses, including a few tears, the departing family then focused on their departure.

The day arrived with bright September sunshine. Jane's chest complaint was under control and she felt comfortable, much to William's pleasure. The last winter had been harsh and he was glad to leave Waterford for that reason. Alan was eagerly looking forward to 'the adventure' as he called the forthcoming voyage.

William had saved fifty sovereigns and Alan had six. William had three hollow leather belts made to stow the coins. They each wore a belt next to their body, under their clothes, just in case of a robbery.

A quick farewell to Jane's parents, luggage and furniture loaded and they were off to Cork via a four-horse carriage. They were the only passengers and the coach stopped twice to change horses. At one stop they had a meal. The trip became boring after an hour or so.

The scenery hardly changed, continuing with farmhouses, green fields, dry rock walls, some sheep and a few ruined castles. The district was historical, but little was written about it. Very few of the locals were educated due to the British attitude towards the Irish born. The catholic priests were the only teachers and they had to do so in secret. Alan had been taught by his mother.

The towns they passed through eased the boredom for a few minutes, the quaint inns with their thatched roofs were perfect reminders of the past. The patrons drinking their Guinness pints sitting outside the inns gave them a polite wave and raised their glasses, saluting the passing of visitors though their village. In fact, they saluted anyone who walked past the inn. It was a tradition in the area; no one knew the origin or even cared. They just did it.

The coach eventually came to a halt outside the shipping agent's office.

The driver shouted down. 'We're here.'

As the William's family disembarked the driver lifted their luggage and furniture onto a four wheeled trolley. He tipped his hat to Jane, climbed back up to the coach seat, cracked the whip and he, his coach and horses continued on their way.

A pleasant red-faced man approached the family and enquired if they were the Chadwick's. They were expected. He explained to them he was the ship owner's agent and he had arranged for them to be accommodated at the inn next door for the next two days, prior to the ship sailing.

They would be visited by the ship agent's doctor for final acceptance but, in their case, it was only a formality as both William and Alan had employment available on arrival in Sydney. The four of them walked to the inn with the trolley, stored their belongings and after they were shown their rooms, the agent departed.

The inn overlooked the large harbour which had ships of all sizes, some at anchor or tied alongside the pier. Which one was theirs? The dockside was a hive of activity: people, trolleys, horse drawn vehicles going to and fro. They wondered – how do they know where to go?

The harbour side streets looked safe in the daylight but at night-time it looked daunting and dangerous. They decided to stay in the inn and go for a walk while it was still daylight.

The next morning a knock on their door was from the promised doctor; a cheerful man who introduced himself and when he saw the teapot on the table asked if he could imbibe. He asked to see their papers and after a quick look at them, he handed them back to William and then sat and chatted about the docks and the ships. After he finished his tea he stood up and bid them, 'Good day and have a good voyage,' and left.

That afternoon the ship owner's agent visited them and advised that they could join the ship the next day at noon or stay in the inn for another day. William decided to join the ship the next day. He was excited to get aboard as soon as possible. Alan shared his enthusiasm, but Jane was apprehensive.

The next morning they were all awake early and made ready for the big day. The agent arrived on time. They loaded the trolley and hired a porter to take it to the ship.

The agent pointed to a small trim three mast sailing ship moored alongside the pier. They walked to the gangway and, after going aboard, were greeted by the first officer who took them to meet Captain Steel. He invited them into his cabin.

As William had been a senior customs officer he was rated as a commissioned officer and he was being treated as such. After the formalities, the captain advised William, his family were the only civilians on the voyage. The remaining passengers comprised a military contingent posted to Sydney to relieve other marines who were due to return to England.

He was further advised he had been allocated the largest two bunk cabin. The other two dual cabins were to be occupied by a military major and his wife and his lieutenant and his wife. The last cabin was a very small one with a single bunk. He turned to Alan saying, 'That will be yours. This ship is only two years old and sails very well. I trust you will enjoy the voyage. I'll see you all for dinner this evening. The first officer will see you to your cabins.'

William's cabin had two portholes opposite their bunks. Jane would have the lower bunk. Their furniture was stowed in the cargo hold and the luggage brought to their cabin.

After they had settled in, they decided to take a stroll down the street alongside the pier. Large warehouses lined the street with small shops between them, selling anything and everything. Surprisingly prices were lower than Waterford's.

On a whim, William purchased two six shot revolvers and gave one to Alan. 'You never know when you might need one.'

Alan hid it under his shirt, held in place by the hollow money belt.

The ship had recently been repainted and looked very smart with its light blue hull. The sails did not look too aged and most of the rigging, ropes and lines appeared reasonably new. The deck had been cleaned by sailors using small sandstone blocks. This was particularly necessary on ships carrying livestock, for hygiene reasons, to ensure any animal droppings were removed. Most of the cargo had been stowed below deck and only a few animal pens were topside.

William went to the quarter deck and looked towards the bow. He could appreciate the sleek design of the vessel and could understand why sailors loved their ships and sailing. He hoped Captain Steel would invite him to the quarterdeck when they were at sea so he could experience the rolling and pitching from the command centre.

The day of sailing heralded the arrival of the military contingent. They could hear the drums of the marching men echoing down the pier. The marines, in three rows, looked impressive, marching in unison, dressed in their red uniforms with white belts. When they arrived at the gangway, the officer leading them called them to 'Halt'.

Captain Steel, in full uniform, walked down the gangway to greet the major who was the commander of the marines. They shook hands and conferred while the ship's first officer met with the lieutenant and together they began boarding the marines. There were also two chartered horse drawn carriages loaded with supplies, guns, ammunition, two light cannon and other miscellaneous supplies.

The marines moved with precision, first to their large steerage accommodation, aft and forward of the quarterdeck. They were issued with hammocks by the sailors, who would later teach the troops how to rig them, how to swing up into them and, more importantly, how to turn over in them and not fall out! They were then lined up on the pier to unload the supplies in an orderly fashion and to stow them in the cargo hold.

Alan stood on the top bow deck watching and admiring the efficiency of the military. The complete loading and stowing took less than two hours.

The time to sail came. The marines were assembled on deck facing the pier. The captain was on the quarterdeck with the first officer and the bosun, issuing orders.

Two row boats had lines attached to the bow and moved the ship away from the pier. The first two sails had been raised and were quickly filling. The pier mooring lines had been released and the ship was moving slowly with the bow heading further away from the pier.

A military band was playing on the pier and a crowd was cheering and waving, some even crying, no doubt friends of the troops.

The tide had turned and was flowing out to sea. Once the ship was moving, the row boats released their lines. The *S.S. Maria* was the only ship moving on the river and was sailing slowly, just above steering control speed.

The marines had been stood down.

The sailors now became much more active as they raised two more sails – climbing the rigging, unfurling sails and cheesing the released lines used at the pier and by the row boats.

There was only a slight breeze; it took a good hour to clear the river mouth. The Chadwicks and the military contingent stood on the deck enjoying the sight of the houses and farms slide by. The green hills and livestock completed the serene picture – a memory to be cherished forever. Some people on the farms waved to them as they passed.

The Chadwicks met Major Dillon and Lieutenant Eden and their respective wives, Rosemary and Freda, at dinner that evening. The women had arrived at the ship an hour after the military arrived. The captain made a short speech of welcome and the major responded.

The group seemed compatible and relaxed. They spoke of their families and general experiences and what they expected looking forward to the voyage and life in the colonies.

The following morning, they were awoken by a bugle call and fifteen minutes later followed by running boots for half an hour. This was to be repeated daily throughout the sailing days of the voyage. Even the major and the lieutenant exercised with the marines. Once a week, a target was towed behind the ship for rifle shooting practise.

Major Dillon kept his men sharp and occupied. They were assigned to work with the sailors, assisting them in menial tasks, such as swabbing the desks, preparing meals and hauling sails. However, the major would not permit them to climb the rigging. Another diversion for the marines was wrestling. Sometimes the sailors competed but generally the marines, who were fitter and better trained, won.

The captain's comment about the ship's performance was correct. It sailed smoothly and gently swayed, without the wallowing, rolling motion of other sailing ships. The hull was deeper and sharper with a longer protruding keel. The ship kept its 'head' and was able to keep its course in rough seas.

Major Dillon was able to appreciate this refinement as he had sailed often to overseas postings during his military career. He had served in the Crimea, India and parts of Africa and in various ships and weather conditions.

Leaving Ireland in the mild September weather was expected to improve Jane's health and, likewise, the anticipated warmer climate of the colonies. The sun and sea air were definitely helping her breathing and colour was returning to her cheeks.

The family wrote letters to family and friends in Waterford most days, ready to post when they arrived in Cape Town. The first few weeks were easy to describe but then the trip started to become monotonous with very little changing from day to day. Even the weather was unchanging. They had trouble not repeating previous events and newsworthy items.

The ship was making good time, the seas were long rolling swells and the wind was light from the starboard quarter. It was good sailing weather. Most of the marines found something to do and occupy their time.

Darts were popular, even though the ship's deck was not exactly the ideal platform to play on. Some read, one even painted seascapes. He was very good and, surprisingly, he was even respected by his uneducated peers and was not being sneered at.

Alan started to study his present from the company 'The Illustrated Book on Coach Building'. Jane had purchased a set of Jane Austin novels and was slowly reading through them. William passed the time playing chess with the first officer, when he was off duty.

They were both good players and improved each other's chess playing ability during the voyage. The women were compatible and socialised most mornings over tea and scones provided by the ship's cook. The women agreed he was a better cook than they were and had a good laugh at this fact.

Major Dillon was an enthusiastic amateur author and had written several books on military tactics. He was now spending most of his time writing of his involvement during his military assignments. He had been in the middle of the Crimea conflict as an artillery officer, in India he had fought in the fierce border battles and in Africa he had seen service against the desert tribesmen. He had been wounded twice, once with a lance in the thigh and another time he had been shot in the arm. He now had a bullet hole in his left upper arm. Fortunately, it had missed the bone. He had been awarded several medals which he wore with pride on parade days.

A ship appeared on the horizon flying the British flag. The S.S. Maria steered to intercept her. The captain asked if anyone had mail for England. Several sailors, a few marines and Alan handed their letters to the bosun who had them transferred across to the other ship at the end of a heaving line. The captains briefly exchanged greetings by megaphone, waved and then sailed on to their destinations.

The ship was approaching the equator and in keeping with tradition, the bosun was charged with organising the Crossing the Line Ceremony. He needed to find a King Neptune and his support team. He was having little luck finding volunteers but was saved by a change in the weather when they experienced a violent storm that lasted three days and the occasion was lost.

They were nearing South Africa. The coastline was visible off the port beam. The ship's side was lined with the marines, sailors and the Chadwicks eager to see land again after several weeks at sea. Table Mountain, the famous landmark towering behind Cape Town, slowly came into view. It had the large flat surface of a mesa, several miles long and three thousand five hundred feet above sea level. They had enjoyed a pleasant voyage with good weather most of the way coming south and it was continuing. The ship was stopping here only to collect fresh vegetables, meat and water for the long trip across the Indian Ocean.

As the ship sailed into Table Bay, Lieutenant Eden went to the quarterdeck carrying a flag. He asked the captain if he would fly the regiment flag to advise the town's military garrison of the contingent's arrival. It was embroidered with the regiment colours. The captain readily agreed. Cape Town had a military garrison on a small hill a mile behind the town with a watchtower overlooking the harbour. It was manned during the daylight hours to monitor shipping movements through the port.

The ship slowly lost speed awaiting the harbour master's boat to come alongside.

Sailors began to climb the ratlines ready to start furling the sails with others busily preparing the ropes and gangway for the ship's berthing. The marines were in full uniform with rifles and bayonets fitted and assembled in line for the major's inspection.

The harbourmaster and the ship owner's agent met with the captain and, after the legal formalities and the ship's paperwork were examined, the ship slowly came alongside. Ropes were cast to the dockside men who looped them over bollards and the ship was slowly moved sideways to the pier. The captain advised all that the ship would sail on the next outgoing tide.

As the gangway was being lowered, Major Dillon could see two army officers standing alongside a four-wheel carriage. He was the first person down the gangway and walked towards them. Lieutenant Eden followed, leading the marines ashore and forming them into line.

Four marines stayed on board to guard their supplies. Major Dillon saluted the local commander, Colonel Miles, who returned the salute. After introductions the colonel was invited to inspect the contingent. They saluted each other and then began to chat informally about the voyage, weather etc.

The colonel invited the contingent to the barracks for a meal and to enjoy a drink. He commented, 'Your arrival is timely. We killed a steer yesterday. There will be steaks all round.'

The road from the pier went past the barracks and was only a twenty-minute march. Lieutenant Eden advised the men and handed over command of the contingent to the sergeant before joining the other officers in the carriage. The carriage then returned for their wives and the Chadwicks who unfortunately had gone for a walk.

As the sergeant assembled the men for the march, a stone was thrown at the marines by one of a group of three drunk men, who then ducked behind a small shed, thinking they had not been seen.

The corporal at the end of the squad had seen them and quick marched from the assembled line with his rifle at the ready. He walked to the shed. The three louts were sitting on the ground laughing. When they saw the marine, they started to rise. He hit the nearest one in the jaw with his rifle butt, the second one in the groin and nudged the third one with his bayonet and told him to start running. He did – very quickly – leaving his mates to their pain. The corporal walked back to his position in line.

The sergeant asked if he had anything to report. He replied, 'All sorted, sergeant'. That was the end of the matter. The marines then marched to the barracks.

After being at sea for so long, the Chadwicks found walking on the dockside strange for the first few hundred yards or so. They had been used to 'feeling' for the deck with the motion created by the sea swell. They strolled by the warehouses and visited the shops, seeking a few souvenirs. They purchased an enormous ostrich egg and a few African native artefacts.

After an hour or so they returned to the ship where the first officer and an army officer greeted them; they had been looking for them. They had been invited to join the colonel and his wife for lunch at the mess.

William had some newspapers in the cabin and quickly collected them. They climbed aboard the carriage and headed to the barracks. They arrived ten minutes before dining time. The major introduced the Chadwicks to the colonel and his wife. His wife then introduced the other wives. William then presented the colonel with the bundle of English newspapers which made the colonel's eyes light up in delight. News from home was always welcomed, even if it was weeks or even months out of date.

After the toast to the Queen and the Regiment, lunch was served. William was sitting next to an Irish officer. When he heard he was from Waterford, he told him a story.

The previous week a drunken sailor, who had missed his ship, fell from the pier into the water and was rescued by two of his soldiers. During his drunken ranting he bragged that he had helped stow away the murderer of the Waterford mayor on a ship sailing to Australia.

The sailor had been gaoled for riotous behaviour and due to his serious allegation was rearrested and put on the next ship to England to stand trial. A statement had been taken from the sailor, in which he described his involvement and positively identified Sean Kennedy with his right leg limp. The statement was then forwarded to the Agent General's Office in London. Alan, who had been listening, just shook his head, thinking, *I hope I never see him again. Australia is a large continent.*

The marines were treated to an excellent meal. Tender meat and fresh vegetables plus a bottle of beer each, what more could a serving marine want! They sat in the sun under the trees surrounding the barracks.

After lunch, the visitors mingled and chatted with the barrack personnel, some who had been in South Africa for nearly two years and were looking forward to their next posting back to England. They could understand William and his family seeking a better climate and a new life and hoped they would find what they were seeking.

The afternoon soon passed and after each of the men was presented with a tankard with the regiment's crest, they made their farewells and departed to the ship.

At the evening's dinner the captain advised the table the ship was ready to sail and would depart at sunrise on the morning's outgoing tide.

It was a misty morning. The wind was gusting from the north east and the waves throwing up little white crests.

The Shearer and the Magistrate

The ship was sailing with a gentle roll as it headed out of the bay, slowly picking up speed.

Alan stood at the steps leading up to the quarterdeck. He looked astern as the waterside buildings slowly disappeared in the morning mist. He wondered – would he come this way again?

Their voyage would cross the Indian Ocean, one of the longest sea routes in the world. They would then enter the Southern Ocean, sailing south out of sight of any land and then parallel with the Australian coast, then around Tasmania and turn due north to Sydney. The captain anticipated arriving within two months. October winds were predominately westerly and generally predictable. that is, without storms. Other ships transited Mauritius, a small island in the middle of the Indian Ocean but the S.S. Maria had no need. The ship was fast, and they had replenished sufficiently in Cape Town. If they needed to visit a port, they would stop at Tasmania's main port – Hobart.

The winds slowly abated, requiring the captain to turn south seeking stronger winds. The further south they travelled the colder it became. More cloud and less sun. It was five days before the winds increased and the ship headed back on a course to intercept their original track. They soon picked up stronger winds and made up the lost time.

A confrontation between a sullen sailor and a marine with a quick temper over access to the heads ended up in a fight, which escalated into a free for all between a dozen men, until the captain intervened. In keeping with maritime culture, he had the bosun give the five sailors ten lashes each and then sent them back to their duties.

The major would not agree to the lashing of his marines. He requested the captain to allow him to lock up his five men in the brig for a week on bread and water. Reluctantly the captain agreed.

This soured the relationship between the two leaders. Captain Steel could not appreciate the different boundaries between a ship's crew and a military platoon, where respect for the leader is paramount, not fear. The lash was not acceptable to the major as he considered it both demeaning and demoralising.

The incident created an invisible barrier between the two groups. William kept to himself and stayed out of the contentious issue. The wives tried to heal the rift without success.

The captain and the major maintained a professional attitude towards each other, but mostly, they communicated through their immediate subordinates. The marines and the sailors now used the mess deck at separate times to avoid any further confrontations.

The voyage progressed without further incident. The strong westerly winds continued and, as anticipated, the west coast of Tasmania appeared on the bow. The lookout alerted one and all with his call of 'Land Ho. Ahead the bow'.

The decks were soon crowded with the ship's passengers, marines and crew, seeing the land gradually appear over the horizon. The long green hills and mist shrouded mountains were impressive. The S.S. Maria turned south and sailed parallel to the coast, then turned east and finally set a course north for Sydney.

A few hours after turning east, settlements began appearing off the port beam. Along the shoreline, with smoke curling above them, were farmhouses behind sandy beaches with small boats fishing in the blue waters. They eventually sailed past Bruny Island and later, in the distance, they sailed past the entrance to D'encastraux Channel leading up to Hobart Town. By nightfall they were on course, heading north to Sydney.

Several days later the coastline of New South Wales appeared off the port side. At dinner that evening, the captain announced that this would be a farewell meal and he had asked the cook to prepare something special to celebrate a safe and sound voyage. He made a short speech and said all long distant ship journeys had an element of danger, mainly from extreme weather conditions or old and unsafe ships. He even had a collision with a whale which nearly sunk his ship. He thanked God for looking after them all and seeing them safely to their destination.

The cook had excelled himself and with the help of a shark caught by a marine, he had prepared a delicious fish dish surrounded by the last remaining fresh vegetables. The dessert was a jam roll coated with sugar. To top off a memorable evening the captain produced a quality aged port. The major stood and proposed a toast, first to the Queen and then a second toast to the captain for his leadership and to his crew for their seamanship.

The closer they came to Sydney the more they saw other ships travelling in either direction. As they approached the harbour entrance, they sailed closer to shore. Suddenly the wind shifted and became an easterly and was moving the ship closer to the cliffs at the entrance. A quick sail change moved them further out to sea. The captain then sailed a long arc to enter the harbour. As they had done in Cape Town, the lieutenant requested that the regiment flag be flown from a mast.

They sailed between the two high cliffs at the entrance to a wide bay, the biggest enclosed bay Captain Steel had ever seen.

All on board crowded the deck, enjoying the view. Farms and buildings lined the foreshore and beyond. The harbour was dotted with boats of all sizes. As they sailed towards the town, a small boat approached them, signalling they wished to come aboard. A customs officer, the ship owner's agent and a military officer from the Governor's office came aboard.

After introductions, Captain Steel, the customs officer and agent went to the captain's cabin to complete formalities. The military officer and Major Dillon went to the ship's bow and became acquainted. He welcomed the marines to Sydney and advised that they were expected, and all was ready for the changeover.

The ship was furling sails and losing speed ready to weigh anchor when the lookout called down, 'Ship astern, ship astern'. A ship was heading towards their stern. The helmsman spun the wheel to turn the S.S. Maria away from its path, but it was too late.

With a resounding crash of splintering timber, the other ship struck them portside, halfway along the quarterdeck and the captain's cabin below. The captain ran to the main deck and ordered the bosun to check for damage below the water line and told the first officer to check for injuries. The other ship had managed to move clear and was moving to an anchorage.

The bilge was taking in water and the bosun ordered two sailors to start operating the pumps.

When he told the captain, he ordered a sail to be collected from the sail locker ready to be slung under the ship as needed.

The major ran to the captain. 'My men are at your command.' The bosun heard him and ordered the nearest five marines to help carry the sail to the quarter deck. The bosun asked for swimmers. The sail was to be pulled under the ship around the hull to slow the water entering the damaged area. Three marines and four sailors stepped forward, undressed and dived into the water. The sail was unrolled and lowered into the water to the waiting swimmers. It took about twenty minutes for the sail to be wrapped tightly around the damaged area.

In the meantime, the shipwrights had been attempting temporary repairs with reasonable success. The cracked timbers below the water line had been forced back into position with blows from large heavy hammers and then doubler planks nailed over them. Over the next few days, the damage would be permanently repaired. The damage to the captain's cabin was secondary to the hull timbers and could wait. The bilge pumps were clearing the water, so the ship was secure and safe from sinking.

The first officer reported two injuries – one was Jane with a badly bruised shoulder when she was slammed into a bulkhead by the force of the collision, and the Sydney customs officer who sustained a deep gash to his head when he tripped in the cabin doorway, hurrying to leave the cabin.

The captain of the other ship came aboard to apologise. He said his rudder had jammed and he dropped anchor to stop his ship, but it dragged on the sandy bottom. The ships shared the same agent so they could sort out any costs. He then left, very embarrassed by the incident. However, both captains agreed it could have been much worse.

The S.S. Maria was moved alongside a pier ready to unload the military supplies. The local garrison provided carriages and troopers to unload and remove the supplies. Within three hours the ship and pier were empty. Major Dillon then assembled his marines in full uniform facing the ship. The captain stood on the quarterdeck watching. Major Dillon saluted and called for three cheers for the captain and the crew. Captain Steel acknowledged the gesture and waved his cap in the air several times – a form of salute! The marines then marched smartly from the pier to their new posting. Captain Steel wondered if he had misjudged Major Dillon.

William and his family thanked Captain Steel for his service and wished him and his crew safe sailing and departed with the now recovered custom's officer. A cart had been arranged for their luggage and furniture which was taken to a bond store for safe keeping. When William mentioned his name to the duty custom clerk he and his family were taken to the supervisor's office and ushered in.

A tall distinguished man in uniform stepped forward, smiling and greeted each of them. 'We have been expecting you. Welcome to Sydney. Please be seated. How was your voyage?'

William was immediately impressed with this man. He replied, 'It was enjoyable, but we're glad to be ashore again.'

'Yes, we all feel that way. I understand that you have accommodation arranged. I know the address. The company is only a mile from this building. Take the office carriage and driver and settle in. I have my gig as well. See me here in two days. I must go now as I have an appointment with the Governor. Goodbye for now.' He shook hands with each of them, called the clerk in and issued a few directions to him and then left.

The clerk took them to the customs carriage stables and gave the driver his instructions. They had only been in Sydney for three hours and were already feeling comfortable in the new environment.

The carriage drive from the custom's building was through narrow and deeply rutted suburban streets. Fortunately, the travel time was only twenty minutes or so. John's stables and workshop were large and imposing. They sat in the carriage for a few moments looking at the stone building. John had done well for himself.

A workman walked across to them. 'Can I help you?'

William replied, 'Yes we're looking for John Chadwick. I'm his brother.'

A voice said, 'Look no further. Here I am. Welcome to Sydney, William.'

William turned to see his brother for the first time in eight years. He was still the same height as William but was a stone or two heavier and suntanned. He looked fit and healthy. They hugged each other for a few moments, then William introduced Jane and Alan.

John led them to a door leading to a stairwell and explained that the ground floor was for the business and upstairs was their home.

The stairs led to a landing in the middle of a large passageway. John pointed and said, 'We live this end; you will have the other end. Come along, I want you to meet my wife, Anne, and stepdaughter, Mavis. Here we are.' He led them into a large open room with a dining setting on one side of the room. On the other side, two women sat embroidering calico pillow covers at a large work bench. They both smiled and stood up to greet William and his family.

John had married Anne five years earlier, a widow who hailed from London and spoke with a distinct cheery cockney twang.

Mavis, her daughter, was born in Sydney. Her father had been a soldier who died ten years ago during a local typhoid epidemic.

After introductions, Anne made tea and, together with some heated scones and jam, they sat down to chat. Questions were asked by all and the afternoon passed happily. John and William were pleased as they could sense their families were compatible, particularly Alan and Mavis. They were the same age and sat chatting about their likes and dislikes. Mavis offered to show him around the stables and off they went.

John and Anne showed William and Jane their rooms. There were two bedrooms and a parlour with a small kitchen, a stove and a water cask. John explained that he collected rainwater from the gutters under the large roof, which drained into a series of casks at ground level. They hand carried pails of water upstairs as needed. John and Anne then left them to unpack and settle in.

Jane looked out of the bedroom window to see the harbour waters in the distance. She knew she would be happy here. Two days later William reported for duty and soon settled into his new position.

Jane offered to be the house cleaner and cook which allowed Anne and Mavis to spend more time making embroidered articles for sale. Alan had several jobs ready for his skills. Studying the manual during the voyage had taught him new techniques which would be valuable. His uncle soon realised he was going to be an asset to his business.

Alan and Mavis were growing closer to each other. They spent nearly all of their spare time together, going for walks to the harbour. They avoided the centre of Sydney. The town smelled of sewage, garbage, animal dung and other unknown odours.

The streets were narrow and the housing varied from shacks to absolute hovels. A block of twenty hovels would shelter around a hundred people. Two rooms being ten feet square, under six feet high with no amenities, leaking roofs and filthy shared backyards. The laneways and alleys were permanent rubbish dumps. One of the worst sights among the riff raff they saw, were the children of all ages, neglected by their destitute parents, who had given up all hope. It was a dangerous place after dark.

A mile from Sydney, it was a different world, with weatherboard and brick homes and contented citizens. Shops were well stocked with items at reasonable prices, compared to London.

Often Alan and Mavis harnessed a pony and gig and explored the immediate countryside. The Aborigines were a surprise. It was not unusual to see a family walk through Sydney Town almost naked. Alan just laughed but Mavis was always embarrassed and looked away.

They gradually grew closer with their common interests and similar attitudes. It was only natural that they would eventually talk of marriage.

Alan was enjoying working for his uncle but if he was going to marry, he felt he needed money to have his own business. He had met many farmers, drovers and shearers when they were having their horses re-shoed or their carts repaired, and he envied their independence. He listened to their stories of how they made their money. Many of the shearers went from shed to shed and, after saving hard, had leased land and settled down, established a flock and then married. Some had started with a hundred pounds and succeeded. Could he do it? How long would it take? Obviously, he was not a recognised shearer. What to do?

He made friends with a shearer who worked his property during the week and did small shearing jobs at a weekend. Alan asked him if he could assist him and teach him to shear. His friend agreed; he would be happy for the company.

Mavis understood Alan's ambition, but she had reservations. After a few months, Alan's friend allowed him to completely shear sheep, not just bellies or crutches. Alan was a natural shearer and was good enough to get a job in a shed; with time he would be a very good shearer. In anticipation of being employed, Alan purchased two hand shears.

Alan and Mavis sat together and pondered. He wanted to marry her, but he wanted more out of life; he wanted a defined future. Eventually she agreed he could have twelve months to achieve his dream – but no more. When they told their parents, they were not impressed.

Two weeks later, John approached Alan to deliver a coach to Merinda sheep station several hours north of Sydney near Newcastle. At dinner that evening Alan said he would not return from the delivery up north and was going to try his hand at shearing for a few months, if he could get employed. He had opened a bank account with the Bank of New South Wales in both his and Mavis's names. He deposited the six sovereigns plus three pounds more he had saved, and three pounds Mavis had. His objective was one hundred pounds. He was unsure how long it would take – he hoped within one year.

The departure day arrived. No one was happy but they all accepted he had a dream for his and Mavis's future and hoped he would succeed. The farewells were quick, a flick of the whip and away went the coach down the dusty road.

His uncle had given him a six-year-old black mare and a bridle and saddle for his use after he delivered the coach. A few clothes, a bedroll and his hollow money belt, including his pistol, were his only possessions.

The road heading north was rough, and the coach needed constant slowing and dodging around pot-holes. He trotted the horse three hours before he stopped for a break. He had a water cask on board which he

The Shearer and the Magistrate

shared with the horse. He gave her the feed bag for ten minutes while he had some fruit and smoked meat for himself. They then continued travelling until dark when he reached a small village. He pulled off the side of the road in front of the store, which was also the owner's residence. He tethered the horse and then lay on the coach floor.

He was comforted by the fact he had the pistol in his belt. He slept well and was woken by the loud crowing of a rooster. He had breakfast at the local inn and, after feeding and watering the horse, he continued north.

The next days were similar – every three hours a break, overnighting in a town and having breakfast at the local inn. He found the Merinda sheep station easily. It bordered the main road and was well signed but not visible from the main road.

For over half an hour he continued up a dusty road to the top of a small hill. Immediately below him he could see several buildings and stockyards. The homestead was a long building with verandas on four sides. A quarter of mile further on was the shearing shed with multiple holding pens and with the workers sleeping quarters and meals area alongside. There were several other buildings – a large stable, storerooms, and other smaller huts. A mile away, a river meandered into the distance.

As he approached the homestead stables a tall sunburnt man waved to him. He walked to Alan, saying, 'Welcome. I recognise my coach. You're on time. I was expecting you this week.' The man was the manager, Fred Green. He inspected the coach and expressed delight with the build standard, together with the ornate paint and leather work. Alan mentioned the coach harness had been included in the price. He was then invited in for tea and a chat, during which the owner casually mentioned that they had just started shearing and asked Alan did he shear. Two shearers had not arrived, and he was looking for replacements.

Alan told him he could shear but had been mainly shearing prize sheep for the agriculture shows. Fred was not concerned; he just wanted a shearer.

He said, 'You can start tomorrow. Go to the shearing shed and report to my foreman; he's the "Boss of the board". Tell him I sent you.'

Alan walked away, praying that he could measure up to the performance of the experienced shearers.

CHAPTER TWO

An Unusual Welcome

The day was cold and miserable. The rain had continued nonstop for four days and as the street was without gutters, the water lay in puddles up to the doorway of the courthouse. James Newton was having a bad day and it was getting worse. He was a member of a legal team prosecuting an alleged offender accused of major fraud. The presiding judge had just ruled vital evidence as non-admissible as it had not been secured continuously under lock and key. The team had been extremely disappointed as they had spent weeks preparing the case submission.

As he left the building, he hailed a passing Hansom cab, stepped out, tripped and fell into a large puddle. He felt like screaming but managed to keep his composure. With what dignity he could muster, he stood up and entered the cab. Fortunately, when he reached his digs – some small inner city rooms that he shared with a friend – he found his friend had already lit the coke burner and, consequently, their two rooms were now warm. After he changed his clothes and had a large whisky, he began to relax.

He sat at the small window looking up the street at the shoppers hurrying about their business. They were unsmiling. Were they so unhappy with the weather, or their lot in life? The rain was continuing. The sky was dark, and the scene looked more miserable. Lately he had been wondering where his future lie? He had been in London for nearly eight years. He had been thinking of a change, but where – Europe, America or the Australian colonies? Australia intrigued him. He would need to explore his options and decide what he wanted to ultimately achieve.

He had a small circle of male friends and a girlfriend – nothing serious but she was good company. The men were mainly work colleagues. They enjoyed a drink and playing cards in this weather. In summer they went boating and hunting in the English countryside and carried on as typical middle-class gentry were expected to behave.

Saturday evening was dance night and an excuse for the ladies to dress formally. Waltzes and circuit dances were the order of the day. Generally, life was good, even if the weather was foul for the majority of winter; but he needed more.

He enjoyed the legal challenges and preparing the briefs for the various alleged offences. Over the years he had been fortunate to have been involved in several High Court crimes that had required extensive research and this had given James a high level of confidence and more experience. This had been noted by his superiors and acknowledged with a modest increase in his salary.

The few days when it was not raining, he would walk to his chambers. The streets were mainly cobblestones but puddles were ever present, and the district always smelled. The so-called sewer system didn't help and when the wind was from the south and blew across the river the stench was even worse.

When he reached his office, which was on the third floor, he considered opening the windows. On some days, if he was lucky, the outside air was tolerable and filtered into the office space.

Their office was several miles west of the London industrial area and normally avoided the worst of the smog and air pollution. James remembered once leaving the office during a bad smog. He was wearing a white shirt and had a long walk to visit a client. When he removed his shirt that night, he was surprised to see the front area, that had been exposed to the open air, was dirty, actually, it was filthy. No doubt this was why there were always a few fellow workers coughing or sneezing. Fortunately he had been spared similar ailments so far.

The streets were always occupied, day and night. Night by the disreputable, the poor, the homeless and the desperate. The ordinary citizen only ventured out in the daylight.

Small shops and alleyway market traders offered their wares, with loud shouts advertising their bargain prices. James and his friends would shop together on a Saturday morning. There were large emporiums several miles away in the centre of London, but the local markets had all they needed.

James was the son of a wealthy north England farmer and Parliamentarian. The family had been yeoman farmers in the district for centuries and, as the only son, they had expected he would follow the family tradition. But he had not been interested in farming, which had disappointed his parents. It had been difficult for them, but they had accepted his decision. They had agreed to send him to be educated at the University of Manchester.

Happy with his parents' support, James selected law and achieved several distinctions on the way to his degree. When he graduated, he was offered a position by a school friend of his father, Albert Armitage Esquire, who had a legal practice in London. Even though James had risen to the daily challenges over the four years and had been acknowledged by the firm, he still felt unfulfilled.

A few weeks ago, over a drink with some friends, one commented that he was going to Australia to serve in the Court of New South Wales and was looking forward to the warmer climate, cleaner skies and fresh air all day.

James recalled the 'filthy shirt day'. He was immediately interested and asked several questions regarding the justice system in the colonies. When he was advised that the Australian colonies' legal systems were based on the English system, James became more interested. The major difference appeared to be land possession laws and control.

James arranged a meeting with the resident Colony of Victoria's Agent General to discuss opportunities that might be available for him with his experience and qualifications. Following his inquiry, he was advised of the dramatic increase of immigration to the colony, due to the discovery of gold. It had generated unprecedented demands on the legal profession. Yes, there were positions in the Victorian Government for persons with his expertise. He was handed a booklet extolling the virtues of the colony. James was impressed.

The Agent General advised accommodation was a problem, but he encouraged James to apply and not let that problem hold him back. His office would arrange his travel details. The accommodation position could change over the next few months.

The thought of a new direction in his life had James thinking of the pros and cons. He had a secure position and future in the legal profession, but he was young and wished to travel. He had no commitments; this was the time to go.

It was a big decision, but many others had gone to the Antipodes before, why not him? Other than his parents, he had no ties. He decided to visit and talk it over with them.

Surprisingly his parents were very supportive. They agreed his youth was his strength and if he did not find the colonies to his liking, he could always return and still pursue his legal career, albeit more knowledgeable and experienced. His parents helped him make up his mind – he would go to Victoria. His father gave him his prized double-barrelled shotgun, a family heirloom.

He spent several days with his parents before he returned to London and even 'Rode to the Hounds' in his red jacket, with his father on the last day. He was sore due to the unfamiliar exercise, noticeably, very tender when he was sitting down. His father presented him with an engraved 'Stirrup Cup' – James Newton Esq – as a going away present and a Bank of England cheque for three hundred pounds.

The departure scene was predictable. His mother cried and he felt the emotion in his father's handshake. He quickly mounted the coach, waved and headed back to London. To the antipodes he was going.

He waited until he received confirmation of his Government appointment before tendering his resignation. Albert Armitage was disappointed but understood the yearning of a young man. He had served two years in India in the British Civil Service and regarded the experience as two of the best years of his life.

He wished him well and said he would always have a position in the firm if ever returned to England. He was then presented with a copy of the transcripts of the previous ten years *Major Criminal Trials of England* – a volume of five books.

James reported to the office of the Attorney General for his travel details. As he was now under their care, he felt more comfortable with his decision to travel to the Antipodes.

The S.S. Locksly would depart in two days. It had been charted by the Victorian Government. It was a three-masted barque, mainly designed for freight. It only had ten passenger cabins; below deck had been loaded with general goods, food, clothing and tooling. He was handed a copy of the manifest with the ship's name, course, captain's name and the passenger list. His fellow passengers comprised, three politicians, two military officers, a doctor, two farmers and a banker.

He had packed two medium sized chests. Books, a few keepsakes and prints with a selection of both winter and summer clothing, including his riding boots and the shotgun. His cabin was small with a single bunk and a sealed round port hole. It gave light but no fresh air. A sailor helped him stow his chests in his cabin and advised him to wedge them between the bunk and the bulkhead for when the weather was rough. It was good advice.

The S.S. Locksly sailed on time and that evening at the captain's table the passengers introduced themselves. Captain Lindsay was a veteran of forty years at sea, in both the Royal Navy and the Merchant Navy, standing six feet tall and weighing over sixteen stone he was an imposing man. He was impressed with his fellow passengers. They all appeared to be professional men, some even leaders in their field.

The farmers were obviously wealthy and were a surprise; they were squatters controlling thousands of acres of grazing and farming land. James listened intently to their stories and how they were handling the problems associated with the distribution or possession of the land especially with the colonies' confusing land legal systems. He made up his mind that first night that this was an area in which he would familiarise himself.

He intended to learn all he could from the two squatters during this voyage. Being employed by the Government, it would be an advantage for him to be aware of the perceived problems from the land holders' point of view as well as the Government's position.

The three politicians, the two military officers and the doctor were all employed by the Victorian Government. The banker was a representative from the Bank of England sent to negotiate a loan to the Bank of New South Wales. Being such a diverse group, mealtime was always an interesting time. The discussions varied from political to bank interest rates to aboriginals and more. James normally just listened, as he was younger than them, unless asked a direct question.

The coast of England slipped by, slowly vanishing into the distance. The sea was rough, and the ship was tacking across wind. Rain was threatening and the skies were darkening.

After dinner they were assisted to their cabins by sailors, some who were bare footed while others wore coiled rope slippers. The ship continued to roll, and it was unpleasant when it pitched up and then came crashing down. James lay on his back with his arms outstretched until he finally dozed off. By morning the seas had abated, and the ship was travelling smoothly, laying slightly over to one side.

Their voyage down the west coast of Africa was surprisingly fast with good sailing weather. As there were only a few passengers and the crew aboard, supply stocks were adequate, they planned to travel a straight course to the Cape of Good Hope at the tip of South Africa. When the ship was in an 'all passengers' configuration, either with troops or convicts and the weather was inclement, it sometimes needed to stop at an intermediate port for supplies as necessary prior to the long voyage heading across the Indian Ocean to Australia.

The S.S. Locksly's first port of call was Cape Town to uplift water, fresh vegetables and fruit, particularly citrus fruit to offset scurvy, for the voyage across the Indian Ocean. The stopover was quick – a handover of mail, an inspection of the hull and pumping the excess water from the bilge. The passengers had only three hours ashore to do some souvenir shopping. The ship sailed out of the harbour on the ebbing tide.

For the first few weeks the weather was good – light breezes and long swells with plenty of sunshine. James enjoyed sitting in the bow with the sun glimmering on the blue waves. Small flying fish would skim across the wave crests. Occasionally a flying fish would leap from the water and land on the mid deck and slide back over the ship's side. The dolphins were the most impressive, to see them diving under and across the bow was a thrill. There were always plenty of them. Sometimes a lone albatross would appear from nowhere and spend a few minutes gliding over and around the ship and then vanish just as quickly into the distant sky. A whale or two had been spotted by the lockout sitting high up in his crow's nest in the rigging. The captain needed to be warned of their presence; he didn't want any collisions.

Alan had started to read through the five books he had been presented with at his farewell – *Major Criminal Trials of England.* He planned to read and digest a book each fortnight. Although he found the trial transcripts very detailed, laborious to read and difficult to absorb, he nevertheless did learn from them. As he had nothing to distract him, he found he retained much of the information he read. The trials varied from murder to fraud and all crimes in between.

One trial intrigued him and encouraged him to keep reading. It concerned a famous fraud carried out by an employee of the Bank of England. He had been transferring monies between branches in a confusing manner and without permission. He had exceeded his authority and mistakenly, it appeared, he had transferred a large sum of money to a bank in France. Then it was found both he and the money had vanished. He was only discovered by accident by a retired bank employee who lived in the same French city the thief had moved to. There was a controversy as to whether he had acted alone. This was the dilemma the court had! Who were the guilty parties? The employee soon gave up his partner in crime and their technique. It was simple – the transferred money did not leave the bank. It was purely a paperwork exercise. His accomplice, a clerk, had written out a bank cheque against a long-time inactive account and hidden the transaction in a morass of records.

The days passed quickly, helped by studying the books and the evening dinner table discussions. Two weeks into the crossing the weather changed dramatically.

One night, James awoke to a flash followed by a crack of lightning, followed by a deafening clap of thunder. This was repeated within five minutes and rain bucketed down. The ship pitched and rolled.

He could hear shouts and running feet. The bosun was ordering the sails to be reefed to reduce the wind effect on the ship. While the helmsman was handling the ship professionally, it was uncomfortable for all. He lay flat on the bunk and stared out the port hole. Alternately he saw the dark clouds billowing in the sky in the moonlight and then the sea water surging with huge white caps. The weather continued for several hours and only abated as the sun appeared over the horizon at dawn.

The clouds were now white and fluffy, and the seas were relatively calm. The wind was still strong and on the stern. The captain advised the passengers that they could expect more bad weather over the next two weeks. The storm had not damaged any of the rigging and the sails were intact, but the galley had become a shamble and it took a day to restore it. Fortunately, no injuries had occurred to the passengers or the crew.

The cook was an ex-Royal Navy rating, an Irish hater and a very hard taskmaster; a big man and a bully. On this trip one of his assistants was Irish and had been given every dirty job in the galley. The Irishman did not complain as he was a fugitive. He was the notorious Sean Kennedy, the assassin of the Waterford mayor. If the cook had known who he was, he would have thrown him over the ship's side. Sean began to build up his own hatred of the cook and bided his time.

Within four weeks they had endured two more bad storms without any undue damage.

The passengers, who were emigrating were given their first sight of Australia, albeit very brief, when they passed the southern tip of the coast of Western Australia. It was barren and treeless and did not impress them. The westerly winds were favourable, and the ship continued to sail close to schedule.

The months of sailing and seeing only fish and birds finally ceased when the west coast of Tasmania appeared on the bow. Not only the passengers but the crew crowded the deck to have a look at the green grey mountains reaching down to the sea. The tops were mostly shrouded in cloud and the sun highlighted the green forests. Only a few small sandy beaches were obvious and a few waterways revealing rivers of this exciting new land. A few wisps of smoke were obvious in the forests but no habitation or people.

The ship turned north east and entered Bass Strait, the sea way that separated the colonies of Victoria and Tasmania. Glimpses of land appeared briefly. The cliffs and rocky outcrops were dangerous and all captains knew of the many ships lost along this stretch of water and stayed well out to sea until they reached the entrance to Port Phillip Bay. Within a few days the ship lined up, ready to enter Port Phillip Bay, waiting to sail in on the ingoing tide. When the tide began to rush into the bay, Captain Lindsay turned the S.S. Locksly and sailed in with the rushing water and when safety through the two headlands, he steered north east for an hour or so and then north up towards Hobson Bay.

Most of the crew went on deck for a view and were engrossed, watching the water swirling and surging around the ship on the incoming tide. In an hour the sea was calmer, and they sailed fast and smoothly. The cook was standing at the bow by himself when Sean crept up behind him and attempted to push him into the sea. The cook sensed his presence, turned and flung out his arm and hit Sean hard on the shoulder. Sean staggered and toppled over the ship's side.

The shout of 'man overboard' was to no avail as the ship was still under the influence of the large water volume flowing in and could not turn and make way against this strong incoming tide. The captain had no choice but to sail on. Sadly, he made an appropriate entry in the ship's log.

Halfway up the bay, he summoned the off duty ship's company and, from a bible, read an appropriate psalm. It was regarded as just another tragedy at sea.

With the sails furled, the ship dropped anchor and the crew began to prepare the cargo for unloading onto barges and relocating to the various warehouses. The customs boat came alongside with the ship's agent and customs officers. The agent introduced himself to each of the passengers, while the captain conversed with the custom's officers to determine what duties would be charged for his cargo.

The agent advised the emigrating passengers that they each had people on the wharf waiting to meet them. The ship's crew had lowered a boat and, after loading their effects on board, they took the passengers to the wharf.

The politicians and the military were immediately approached. The farmers and the doctor went their own way, leaving only James and the banker standing by themselves. A young man about James's age, approached him and enquired if he was James Newton. He introduced himself as Richard Nelms, a court official. He had been assigned to help James settle in. He had anticipated the volume of James's luggage and had brought a cart.

Richard took him to the police barracks where accommodation was provided, and he was shown where the dining room was located. He said, 'I'll return at nine a.m. tomorrow and take you to our offices. I trust you will settle in comfortably. Goodbye for now.'

The Shearer and the Magistrate

After dinner, James had an early night. His room was on the first floor. Through his large window he could see over a parade ground and, further on, he could see a river flowing slowly with boats busily travelling between the many shore landings.

The next morning, Richard arrived on time and gave James a running commentary of the streets and major buildings of Melbourne. Several bluestone buildings were impressive. Shops, many cottages and others were substandard. Only a few roads had been formed. Potholes were everywhere and footpaths virtually undefined. Richard said there were plans for the roads to be improved and these were due to start within two months. He pointed to the substandard buildings and advised they were required to be improved or removed by the end of the year.

They stopped in front of a large bluestone building suitably embossed in gold paint, 'Court of Victoria'. They were greeted by a uniformed attendant. Richard took him to the administration office and introduced him to the chief clerk, Mr Raymond, a tall unsmiling sombre man. After the normal pleasantries he was briefly shown to his office and then taken to meet the chief magistrate.

Michael Lynch was a Londoner with a broad accent. He motioned James to a seat and called for tea. He said he was delighted to have him finally arrive. He had been expected two weeks ago.

The chief magistrate advised that he had been impressed with James's experience and he had decided to appoint him as a magistrate. 'You will be of more value to me in the field than in an office.' He told James that he would be given a week to settle in and explore Melbourne. The following week he would be sworn in as a magistrate and then he would accompany another magistrate to familiarise him with the local procedures and the courts. Afterwards he would be assigned small cases in Melbourne and eventually he would perform visiting magistrate duties in the country. Although there was a backlog of cases, James would not be rushed. It was up to him to set his own pace during his early days.

The chief clerk accompanied him to his office. James asked him to send a person to collect his books from his room. The chief clerk advised him he was entitled to his own clerk, but he agreed to arrange the collection and walked away.

The office was cosy with a small heater in the centre. The window faced the west and would provide afternoon sunlight. The desk was large with several pigeonholes. A bookshelf, three comfortable chairs and a small conference table completed the furniture. Having his own office was a bonus and a first. In London he had shared office space with five others. He unpacked and stowed his books and sat down to plan his next few days.

Richard Nelms dropped by his office at noon and asked if he could help him in any way. James took the opportunity to invite him to lunch so that he could ask him about becoming familiar with Melbourne.

He found Richard a friendly and affable person. He had served in the British Army as a rifleman. Being of a similar age they communicated on the same plane. Richard obtained a map of the area and after pointing out specific items and areas of interest and necessity, he looked at James enquiringly.

James nodded and thanked him. 'I'll walk the town as it is compact, well laid out and it will help me to remember the district.'

Richard went back to work, and James started exploring with Richard's map. He spent the rest of the afternoon walking and looking.

During the week he walked the town three times. He admired the bluestone government and business buildings. In such a few short years the town was growing, and it showed it had a positive future. The people also were of interest. They ranged from farmers – both wealthy and struggling, sailors from all nations, men in uniforms of all colours, shopkeepers, businessmen and the unfortunate ones who were down and out.

The streets were busy during daylight hours. Horse drawn vehicles of all sizes with painted company signs and solitary riders travelled the roads. He wondered how their wheels survived the numerous potholes, or maybe they didn't. There was no doubt the town was vibrant and trading. Gold had made a few Victorian's wealthy, and now it shared its prosperity.

The second week he went to the chief magistrate's office to complete his training assignment.

The chief magistrate performed the formal swearing in procedure and introduced him to his mentor, Walter McLeod. James then mentioned that he would like Richard Nelms to be his clerk. The chief agreed. When Richard was told of his new role, he nodded and smiled and thanked James.

James soon understood the routine. The procedures and processes were virtually the same as the English. Even the court layout was similar but a little smaller. The charges were a mixture of criminal and civil. They attended a robbery trial that took two days and five civil litigations. None were complex and he followed the proceedings without trouble. He was ready to preside on his own and the chief magistrate agreed.

Richard came into his office with two folios from the chief clerk and advised they were his first two cases. The first was an assault of a constable and the second an alleged theft of livestock.

The first case was scheduled for ten a.m. and the second at one p.m. He hoped the first case was uncomplicated and could be finished before noon; he didn't want to overrun his first case.

'The court will rise,' greeted James as he took his seat. The case was straight forward. The alleged offender admitted to being drunk and hitting the constable once. It was the offender's first offence. He was only twenty years old and the young man was very remorseful. He was convicted and fined two pounds and given a caution.

The afternoon case was a bit confusing as two persons had bills of sale for the same described animal dated the same day. The brand had been defaced and the previous owner was overseas but had submitted a letter of explanation but no other information. The lawyer representing the previous owner was in court.

James asked to see the letter and then compared the handwriting. One bill of sale was supported by the handwriting in the letter. James awarded the horse to this person. The person with the false bill of sale was taken away by the police. He later admitted his attempt to defraud. James was happy with his first day in his own court.

The weeks rolled on and he was now being given assignments outside of Melbourne.

James was unexpectedly called into the chief magistrate's office without warning. He had not seen him for over three weeks and was curious as to why. He was motioned to sit down.

The chief magistrate started. 'James, I have a rather awkward case for you in Geelong. An affray between four grammar students and five apprentices. It sounds like a simple street fight, but it, unfortunately, caused minor injuries to a young mother and a lady gig driver.

'The police were called and the nine were arrested,

even though they were in their late teens. It now gets messy. Two of the students have had their charges withdrawn after admitting their involvement in writing. I want you to handle the case with kid gloves. The two students who had their charges withdrawn are sons of the two wealthiest families in the western district and are both related to a government minister.'

James looked at him. 'Have the police given the court a reason yet?'

He shook his head. 'No, I left that to you. You will need to be on your toes. The defence counsel will probably raise the question. Good luck and take Nelms with you. You may need a friend.'

The case was scheduled for the following Wednesday. They allowed a full day to travel to Geelong and Tuesday to do some research.

Richard was at James's door at eight a.m. with a gig ready for their first trip to Geelong. The town was situated on Corio Bay about fifty miles southeast of Melbourne.

It was a pleasant journey with stops at Werribee and Little River. The countryside was relatively flat but low hills to the west gave an interesting perspective to the view.

On arrival at the courthouse, the clerk showed them to their office and directed them to their hotel. They both had an early night to ensure they would be ready for what might challenge them the next day.

When they arrived at the courthouse, they were advised that they had visitors waiting for them. This was unexpected but they were ready for the unexpected. They had just opened their folios when a knock on the door preceded the door clerk. He asked if they were ready for the three gentlemen requesting an audience.

James nodded. 'Show them in.'

Three men entered and the first proffered his hand. 'Good morning and thank you for seeing us without an appointment. I'm Milton Tom and these are my clients, Mr Stockland and Mr Darcy.'

James acknowledged their handshakes and introduced Richard as his clerk. They seemed surprised at James's youth. He gestured them to be seated. 'To what do I owe this visit?'

He had recognised the names of Stockland and Darcy as the names of the two students who had retracted their guilty statements. He thought, *Well, here we go.*

The lawyer started. 'No doubt you are aware of the facts of the case from start to finish. So, I won't bore you. Our concern is how the court will view the withdrawal of the original statements of Mr Stockland and Mr Darcy.'

'The court is here to pass judgement on the charges presented by the prosecutor, nothing more nothing less,' replied James.

The answer puzzled the trio. They looked at each other, unsure what to say next.

James took the initiative. 'If that is all, gentlemen, I bid you, good morning. I have a very busy day in front of me.' He then stood up followed by Richard, who had been recording the conversation. The trio followed suit and stood up.

They all shook hands and went about their business.

Richard laughed. 'When you gave them that answer it took the wind out of their sails. They were ready for an argument.'

James, too, was happy the way the meeting had gone. Now was the difficult one – the district police inspector's response and why.

The district inspector had been in Geelong for ten years and was highly respected. He was due to retire at the end of the year. He knew that the withdrawal of the statements would cause questions to be asked. When he had agreed to the request, it seemed a simple matter involving a few juveniles. In hindsight, he was wrong, very wrong!

When his secretary advised him that he had two court officials asking to meet with him, he nodded to bring them in. He stepped from behind his desk to greet them.

He was surprised at their young age. After the introductions he called for tea and they all sat at a small table. Small talk about the Geelong district soon gravitated to the next day's proceedings and the issue of the withdrawn statements arose.

James came to the point. 'It is not an issue for me, as I am only dealing with the charges presented, but you must be aware that the lawyers of the others may raise the subject. I admit that I have been asked to find out why they withdrew their statements. However, at this moment I do not want to know, in case it could affect my decision. Before I leave, I may wish to speak with you again.'

The inspector nodded and replied, 'I understand your position. Thank you for being candid.'

James and Richard shook hands and left. They stopped at a tea room and discussed the day.

Richard said, 'I was getting writer's cramp, but I think I got everything. I'll rewrite it more neatly back at the office.'

The day of the court case saw a larger crowd than normal. The court proceedings progressed as expected. The defendants were identified and asked to plea. The seven all nervously pleaded guilty. The prosecutor then read out the charges and described the incident. Each of the statements agreed in content.

'One of the defendants had red hair and was laughed at by one of the other groups. Then he called him an Irish twit. He took umbrage. A push led to a shove, culminating with a punch and they all joined in the fight. We have been unable to identify who threw the first punch. I doubt if anyone knows. The lady with the pram was leaving a shop when one pugilist tripped and tipped the pram over. He immediately went to her aid and apologised. At the same time another lad stumbled onto the road and startled a young filly in a gig. The driver was a farm lass and was able to jump off as the filly galloped across the road and swung the gig into a shop window, breaking it. The police were called and immediately arrested the nine alleged offenders and took them to the Geelong Police Station.'

James interrupted the prosecutor. 'The defendants just waited around for the police to arrive? They didn't leave the area?'

The prosecutor looked towards a uniformed constable.

James motioned him to come forward and stand with the prosecutor. 'Can you answer my question?'

The constable replied, 'No, they did not run away. They were all helping clean up the broken glass from the roadway.'

James nodded and dismissed him. He asked the prosecutor to describe the injuries of the two women.

'The young mother had a slightly bruised right shoulder and the farm girl a twisted left ankle. Neither was required to stay overnight at the hospital. The gig had a broken wheel spoke and the filly was sound.'

James asked the defendants' lawyers to present their defence. Neither lawyer presented a defence due to the written statements previously presented in court.

However, both lawyers presented similar character references from noted persons and said the lads came from good and stable homes. They had not been in trouble before and they all played in local sports clubs. It seemed they wanted the trial over quickly.

James asked if they were going to call any witnesses. They said 'no' and sat down.

The prosecutor stood and advised James, 'If that is so, that completes our case.'

James called an adjournment until the next day. He had heard enough to reach a verdict.

He called Richard to him and asked him to see if the other two lads were in court and to bring them, their parents and their lawyer to his room for an informal talk. When they arrived, he explained that the evidence from the witnesses was overwhelming and that the two boys had been involved in the altercation, as they had admitted in their statement.

'Why did they withdraw it?' James looked to their lawyer to respond.

The lawyer hesitated.

A woman's voice spoke. 'Because they will lose their scholarships if they are found to have breached the school's code of conduct.'

James asked, 'But I understand they weren't wearing a school uniform and the charge sheets do not say anything about the school.'

The woman continued. 'We also paid the costs for the window and some compensation.'

The lawyer tried to stop her talking.

James now knew why the statements were withdrawn.

The farmers were looking uncomfortable and looked at each other.

He asked Richard to go to the district inspector and pass on his regards. He wished to speak with him as soon as possible. Richard and the district inspector arrived within the hour.

James asked him if he was on good terms with the local newspaper editor. He explained that up to now no mention had been made of the school and said it would be in all parties' interest to ensure this situation continued.

The district inspector nodded his understanding and left immediately. Later in the afternoon he returned and advised that the newspaper would not have a reporter in attendance at the hearing the next day.

James sat down, looking at the audience. They were eagerly waiting for him to begin and, more so, waiting for his verdict. He started by asking the prosecutor and the two defence lawyers if they wished to speak. They each declined his offer.

After shuffling a few papers, he began. 'The young men before me all are career orientated. Victoria is a young country and needs people like them to help the colony develop.

'Affrays, unfortunately, occur often between young men. I do not condone them but it's a fact of life. I have also been advised that no other issues are outstanding. I have watched their excellent behaviour during the hearing. Further they have each shown genuine remorse and have written letters of apology to the affected parties. Your decisions to stay and help clean up the glass was commendable. I have, therefore, decided that no conviction will be recorded, and no penalty will be imposed. You may go.' The verdict was greeted with cheers and claps. James stood, bowed and left the room. They planned to leave within the hour.

The district inspector came to see them leave. He asked, 'You know some of the story and have guessed that sometimes results are achieved differently in the bush. As you know, I am retiring in four months so I am interested in what you will report.'

James replied, 'I will eventually make a report, but it may take a month or so. My report will not be critical and, yes, I am learning the colonial country ways. Your superiors will possibly investigate but it won't hurry my report. I feel sure you will be able to delay your possible investigation for four months. I wish you well and now I must away. Goodbye.'

When he reported to the chief magistrate, he was surprised to find that he already knew of his verdict.

He laughed. 'I knew an hour ago. Several people were nervous of the outcome and needed to know immediately. You're in good favour because of your colonial verdict. The district police inspector will be questioned eventually but it may take a while. The investigative officer has quite a large backlog. Take a few days off to complete your report.'

James shook his hand and returned to his room.

James's next assignment was a series of hearings throughout central Victoria. They varied from attempted armed robbery, family violence to arson. He took Richard with him as he had troubles previously with unsupportive local staff when he required some research of local evidence and general information. Richard could devote his time collecting this data and leave James to prepare for the hearing and familiarise himself with the charges.

They arrived in the town where he was to hear an armed robbery case involving violence. When the coach trip became monotonous, James used the remaining time to read through the case files Richard had been provided with in Melbourne.

Three armed bushrangers had bailed up a coach and guns had been fired. Unfortunately for the robbers, the robbery had been interrupted by four travelling drovers arriving with their dogs. The robbers rode away but the horse of one robber fell and the drovers captured the youngest brother, John Marsh. They took him to the nearest police station where he was locked up, pending trial. The statements made by the drovers were witnessed by the local senior constable and were now in James's briefing papers.

James and Richard checked into the biggest hotel.

When the young receptionist realised who they were she said, 'Good. I hope you teach young Marsh a lesson. The family are a bunch of outlaws, in and out of jail. They have been a menace around here for years and their policeman school mate does nothing.'

When James told her of the hearing time she said she would see that the other hotels knew. This would ensure the word got around town. James was surprised at the last comment but did not answer.

They then strolled to the police station.

A young constable stepped forward. 'What can I do for you gentlemen?'

James introduced himself and Richard. They were shown to an office where a short stocky senior constable sat. He looked up and asked, 'Yes? ' When James and Richard were introduced, he started and said, 'You were not due until tomorrow and the hearing was planned to be held the next day.'

James replied, 'We have commitments in other districts and changed our schedule. I will hear the case tomorrow at ten a.m.'

The senior constable stuttered, 'No, that is not possible. The courthouse will not be ready.'

James sensed a problem was looming and decided to be firm.

He turned to Richard. 'Courthouse? Find the Mechanics Institute and arrange for our use from nine thirty a.m. until noon, advertise it on their noticeboard and then meet me back at the hotel.' He then faced the still sitting senior constable and ordered, 'I want any paperwork that you have on the case sent to my room by five p.m. Good afternoon and remember to have yourself and the alleged offender at the court by nine forty-five a.m.' He nodded to the constable and walked out of the police station.

The comment made by the receptionist concerned him. He would definitely follow this up. When he met Richard at the hotel, he sent him to speak with the alleged offender's lawyer and advise him of the change of the court hearing. The lawyer advised Richard that the alleged offender intended to enter a guilty plea. James had gained a reputation of leniency with guilty pleas.

The clock showed five twenty p.m. and the paperwork had not arrived. Suddenly the constable appeared, somewhat agitated. He reported, 'The senior constable was unable to find the papers but said he would search for them again first thing tomorrow.' James could see that the constable was uncomfortable. He invited him to sit down.

He said, 'I appreciate your loyalty and that this is a small town, but I need to know about the Marsh family. What can you tell me about them?'

The constable nodded. 'Yes, you need to know. They have lived here all their lives. The men are constantly in and out of jail for being drunk, brawling, cattle theft and are despised throughout the district and they bully the senior constable. He can't control them. The other two brothers and the Irishman are supposed to arrive in town in two days and I'm sure there will be trouble. The sooner the hearing is over, and the brother is moved, the better for all. I'd like to go. I don't want people seeing me talking with you here.' James nodded; the talk was over.

After dinner James and Richard went through the paperwork in their folio to prepare for the hearing. They had the original charge sheet, eight witness statements, a record of the Marsh men's criminal history plus a rambling and confusing report by the senior constable. A prosecutor had been assigned. If he was not there by ten a.m. Richard, who was a court official, could assume that role.

After breakfast, the two went for a stroll around town. It was a typical country town. People were up and around early, horses and carts were lining the street, shops were open and busy doing business. Many politely nodded 'good morning'. They returned to the hotel and packed their travel cases ready to leave on the one p.m. coach.

The Mechanics Institute Hall was half full of interested residents. The bench and chairs had been set up by the hall committee. They had obviously done this before.

James and Richard went via the jail to ensure that the police and the alleged offender were organised. Surprisingly they saw the senior constable riding quickly in the opposite direction heading out of town. Entering the police station, they saw the constable throwing his hands into the air.

When he saw James, he complained. 'The senior constable said he had been told of a robbery in the hills and to tell you he thought it was more important than today's trial and to delay it until tomorrow.'

James told the constable, 'The hearing will go ahead. I don't need his presence. Get the prisoner and bring him to the Mechanics Institute Hall.'

The constable said, 'That's my problem. He has the key to the cell. I can't open it.'

The three of them went to the cell. James pointed to the hinges. 'Go and get the blacksmith and have him remove the hinge pins. A few blows with a sledgehammer will pop them up and out. I'll delay the hearing until you arrive.'

The constable and the prisoner only arrived a few minutes late. Richard called the court to order and read out the charge sheet. 'John Marsh, you are charged with armed robbery.'

He asked Marsh, 'How do you plea?'

Marsh answered nervously, 'Guilty, Your Honour.'

James looked to the defence lawyer, who stood. 'As you can see, Your Honour, my client is a young man of eighteen years and has only had one other conviction, that of brawling. Generally, he is gainfully employed as a contract timber cutter. He is in a relationship of three years and has shown remorse. He is the youngest of three brothers. Perhaps their undue influence has caused his waywardness. I believe this is a wake-up call for him to decide his future and as he has pleaded guilty perhaps a lenient sentence would be appropriate, Your Honour.'

James had been looking at Marsh during the speech. He looked his eighteen years and after reading the crime history of his older brothers he thought their influence could have contributed to him now being in the dock. He asked the prisoner if he wished to say anything on his own behalf.

Marsh took a deep breath. 'I know I have done wrong. I have upset my mother and girlfriend. I promise I will try not to break the law again.'

James called a ten-minute break. He and Richard went to the back room and sat down. They were convinced the youth was being truthful, but he had been involved in armed robbery. He would get a jail sentence, but how long? His brothers would have been given ten years. James decided to sentence him to two years. A very lenient sentence.

When they returned to the court the babble from the crowd immediately stopped. There was silence. They could even hear a horse whinny outside.

Richard called the court to order and asked the prisoner to stand. James first looked at the people seated. He sensed they wanted a jail sentence just because the prisoner was a Marsh. The prisoner was standing with his hands tightly gripping the front of the dock.

James spoke, 'Mr Marsh, I have accepted your lawyer's comments and I believe that you have learnt a lesson. The charge of attempted armed robbery is serious. However, I believe the toxic environment you have grown up in is the prime cause for you to be standing where you are today. I have ruled that you will be jailed for a period of two years. Constable, remove the prisoner.' James stood up and, with Richard, left the court.

Some of the observers were smiling, others nodding, and the remainder scratching their heads, wondering if it was the correct sentence or not.

James and Richard went back to the jail. Richard to complete their paperwork, while James wrote two identical letters, which puzzled Richard.

The constable had handcuffed the prisoner to the cell bars and was waiting to talk with James. He looked at him and said, 'We will take the prisoner with us to our next town which has a large jail. It will save you from any more pressure from your senior constable.'

The coach arrived on time and the three boarded, ready for their trip to the next town.

As James boarded, he handed a letter to the constable to be given to the wayward senior constable. Richard smiled; he guessed what the contents would be.

The senior constable arrived back in town around three p.m. The constable was talking with a friend outside the police station. He asked, 'How was today?'

The constable replied, 'The court hearing was held, and the prisoner has gone'.

Before he had a chance to explain, the senior constable said, 'Thank God for that. I didn't think he would get off.' He walked quickly into the police station and asked to be told about the court hearing. As he listened, he was dismayed, and when told that the prisoner had been taken to another jail, his first thoughts were, *How would the Marsh's react?* They had asked him to delay the hearing until tomorrow when they were due to arrive. They had planned mischief during the proceedings, but he didn't know just what.

The constable then handed him James's letter.

Apprehensively he opened the envelope as he sat down, and started to read. He suddenly realised the enormity of his mistake in not supporting the magistrate. The letter was addressed to the 'District Inspector' and listed four of his failings, briefly they were:

a. His lack of respect for an officer of the court
b. Loss of court files
c. Being obstructive, i.e. advising the non-availability of a court room
d. Retaining the cell key when he knew it was required.

He now had problems coming from two directions and expected the worse. Three days later he was waylaid and severely assaulted and four weeks later dismissed from the police force. It could have been worse; he could have been jailed. At the time the Victorian Police Force had many similar incidents of poor policing and didn't want any more bad publicity. They were slowly identifying dishonest and under performing constables and replacing them with men of good character. It would take time.

During the coach trip, James asked Marsh, 'What did you know about the mysterious Irishman?'

Marsh replied, 'I didn't like him. He's always angry and nasty. He came down from Sydney with some drovers and had an argument with them and was sacked. He then came to our farm for a job. I don't know why my brothers mix with him. He never works; just lazy and idles around. I think he's hiding from the law. He talked my brothers into the robbery. He said it would be easy, seeing they would be armed. He didn't expect to be challenged by the drovers. He gave me the job to hold the horses.'

James felt confident John Marsh had learnt his lesson.

James and Richard read the briefs on their next case – that of family violence. Ironically, the plaintiff was a male.

He had accused his wife of grievous bodily harm. Namely, she hit him twice with a meat cleaver, chopped off two of his fingers, broke his right arm and inflicted a deep laceration.

The reason was not given in the papers. James thought this case would be a bit different for a change. Richard said it was the first case he had heard of where a male was the plaintiff in a family violence charge.

Richard had sent a letter by coach to the local police station, advising that James and he would arrive a day earlier than planned and, if possible, for the interested parties and their representatives to be available tomorrow for a two p.m. hearing.

The coach arrived on time and James and Richard took the prisoner to the police station and handed him over to the duty constable. After introducing themselves, the senior constable stood up and walked from behind his desk to shake their hands. He advised that the parties would be available for tomorrow and handed over the file with the case details. The reception was entirely different from the previous police station.

James and Richard retired to their hotel accommodation and read the file. The reason for the attack was surprising. Mr and Mrs Embry had been married for over five years, had no children and leased a three-hundred-acre property where they ran two hundred sheep and fifty breeding cattle, on prime land. She was a recluse and rarely came to town; her husband did a fortnightly shopping run. The attack seemed to be without reason. The husband obviously wanted his day in court. She had been released to her sister's care with a few conditions. The main one being, not to approach her husband under any circumstances.

The court was almost empty. The couple were not well-known and the case was of little interest to the local community. The plaintiff, the accused, and their representatives were seated. The senior constable would be acting as the prosecutor.

James looked at Mr and Mrs Embry. She was a big woman and though she had her head down she appeared very angry. Mr Embry was a small man and was sitting at the back of the court, almost hidden. Richard called the court to order and silence prevailed. James asked the prosecutor to read the charge sheet.

He read, 'Mrs Ellen Embry, you are charged with causing grievous bodily harm to Mr Bill Embry.'

James asked Mrs Embry, 'Do you agree with the charge as read?'

The prosecutor asked, 'How do you plea, guilty or not guilty?'

At this moment Mrs Embry spotted her husband and she released her anger. Her lawyer had previously tried to calm her down. She glared at her husband and answered, 'Yes, I'm guilty, and I bloody meant to kill him, and if I get the chance again, I will. Yes, I will kill him next time.'

The prosecutor looked at James, waiting for him to respond. James turned to Mrs Embry's lawyer and asked, 'Do you wish to comment on her response?'

The lawyer shook his head. 'Your Honour, she won't listen to me. I've tried several times to calm her down. I don't know why she wanted me here today.'

James said, 'Thank you. Remove Mrs Embry to the back of the court. I would like to hear from Mr Embry. Please come forward and be sworn.'

Mr Embry stepped forward and was sworn. James asked him to tell him what happened on the fateful day.

He started by saying, 'My wife has not been right in the head for the last few months. She has become increasingly more violent.

'On the day of the attack I told her I had decided to cancel the farm lease and go my own way. She could go and live with her sister. I had had enough of her anger. She went berserk and attacked me with the cleaver and left me lying on the kitchen floor. I managed to wrap my hand and arm in towels to stop the bleeding and strap a belt around it and then ride to the doctor. I want nothing more to do with her. I have given her sister fifty pounds. After today I am leaving this town for good. If anyone wants to contact me, they can do so via the local church minister. He has agreed to keep my address confidential.' James nodded and Mr Embry returned to his seat.

James thought for a while and then ordered that the defendant, who was still disturbed, to be committed for a psychiatric evaluation in Melbourne. He said, 'I see no reason to progress this hearing any further due to what I have seen and heard today. The hearing is adjourned indefinitely.'

Meanwhile, a furious Mrs Embry tried to leave the rear court seat and attack her husband again. She was still yelling after the police handcuffed her and dragged her from the court to a cell. The constable sent a message to the local doctor asking him to sedate her.

Richard closed the court and the two of them returned to the hotel for afternoon tea. The paperwork was duplicated – one for the local record and one for Melbourne.

James felt sorry for the prisoner. Even with his limited knowledge of life in the bush, he could imagine the loneliness and harsh climate would be testing enough, but to have a mental problem as well? Mr Embry looked a tough farmer and a survivor, but he had reached the limit of his tolerance and made a life changing decision.

The constable sent Mrs Embry on the next prisoner's wagon to Melbourne. Four days later she was dead; she hanged herself. The verdict was 'Suicide – Death by hanging due to an unsound mind'. The case was marked – closed.

The next morning, they handed over the paperwork, thanked the police for their support and boarded another coach to the next town. The arson case paperwork revealed a case of malicious damage to several haystacks by a disgruntled farm hand. It appeared to be straight forward. The two of them expected to be back in Melbourne within two days.

As normal, on arrival they checked into a hotel and then visited the police station. They found that the alleged offender had skipped town and vanished. James issued a warrant for his arrest and went to walk back to the hotel with Richard, when, suddenly, they were confronted by three armed men. Richard went to pull out his revolver but was shot in the shoulder and collapsed to the ground. James's arms were tied up, and he was bundled into the back of a cart and covered with a horse blanket. The cart and the two horsemen headed out of town towards a dense forest.

James had not realised the anger of the Marsh gang. They had been searching for him and Richard since they found out that the senior constable's delaying tactics had not worked. They had attacked and injured the senior constable and if the constable had not arrived on the scene with a double-barrelled shotgun, he may have been maimed forever.

The cart bounced along the road and gave James a very unpleasant journey. He wondered what this was all about as no one had spoken to him yet. After several hours the cart stopped, and the blanket was removed. James found himself being peered at by three bearded men. One finally spoke. 'Do you know who we are?'

James answered 'No, why, should I?'

That answer was unexpected 'We're the Marsh gang.'

James didn't answer.

'We have kidnapped you and will swap you for our brother, John. What do you say to that?'

James replied, 'Well, what do you want me to say?'

This further confused the gang as they had expected him to plead for his release. The three walked away and, after a few minutes, lifted him from the cart. They were at a small farm. The sun was setting, and the gang decided to have a meal. Fried meat, potato, damper and a cup of tea was the order of the day and was enjoyed by all except the Irishman; all he did was complain.

James picked him as the most dangerous of the three. He had a nasty streak in him. He threatened to hit James, but the others stopped him, and he walked away and sat by himself, staring into the forest.

The next morning, they decided to ditch the cart and only use the horses. It would be easier to travel into the hills. They made good time and believed they could not have been followed. That night they camped in an open clearing in the forest and tied James to a tree. They did not post a lookout.

CHAPTER THREE

Gone Shearing

Merinda's manager, Fred Green, was a large jovial man but he looked to be a tough, no nonsense person. He told Alan to put his horse in the home paddock, stow his gear in the tack room, then go to the sleeping quarters and select a bunk. He was to join the shearers in the meals room and introduce himself. He pointed towards the largest building at the end of the row of buildings, waved and walked to the homestead.

Alan followed Fred Green's instructions and entered the sleeping quarters. The shearers had this building for themselves. The other shearing shed workers were housed separately. The building was built similarly to the shearing shed except it was not raised. He waited until the shearers returned and asked one of them to be shown to a spare bunk. He was pointed to a vacant one with a window above. Alan was intrigued by the clothes of the shearers, a pair of moleskin trousers and a singlet or a flannel shirt and no socks seemed to be normal attire. Some were barefooted or had handmade slippers or wrappings on their feet.

The Shearer and the Magistrate

Alan awoke early and lay in bed, listening to the crowing of a distant rooster. At sun-up, *Merinda Station* came alive. The sleeping quarters' door burst open and in walked the 'Boss of the Board' shouting, 'Rise and shine. Wakey! Wakey! Time to rise and shine'. Fifteen shearers, including Alan, quickly dressed. After a quick wash at the horse trough and a filling breakfast, he followed the other shearers into the shed.

The boss took Alan to an end shearing bay and asked him to shear a few sheep, to see if he would agree with the manager's decision to hire him. Nervously Alan dragged a medium sized ewe from the adjacent pen, rolled her onto her rump and, with his hand clippers, started shearing. After he had shorn three sheep, he looked at the boss. He nodded and said he was a bit slow, but he was a good shearer – no cuts or nipples severed. He had the job.

Alan now had a chance to look around the shearing shed, or as some called it 'the wool shed'. It was about one hundred and thirty feet long and built on wooden piles a few feet from the ground. The shed had wooden frames and was enclosed with corrugated iron sheets. The floorboard slats each had a one-inch gap between them for the sheep dung and small rubbish to be swept into and below to the ground. At one end of the shed was a large holding, or sweating bay, to keep the sheep from the weather before they were moved into the shearing pens. At the other end of the shed were the wool tables where the wool classers separated the wool into various grades. Clothing or combing wool were the most valuable; the bellies, locks and pieces were of little value.

Between the holding bay and the classer's area, were the shearers' positions or the 'board', as it was called. The board could cater for eight shearers on each side but today there were only fifteen shearers. The sheep were driven from the holding pen by a rouseabout and down a centre race or passageway to the catching pens for the shearers to drag out and shear.

After shearing, the sheep were pushed out through a small door to an outside holding paddock.

Alan was impressed with the shed size but not with the heat from the iron sheeting.

Before Alan had decided to become a shearer, he had considered erecting fences and rabbiting. He had compared their wages, possible savings and their lifestyles. A rabbit trapper/shooter could earn big money, but it would be a solitary life by oneself. He had been told some developed mental problems and ended up becoming hermits. This was not for him.

He had met a few fence builders. They normally worked in fours, one digging, another installing the posts or poles, while the other two cut the posts or poles or drew the wires. The problem was that they needed to be compatible. Working and living in each other's pockets for twenty-four hours a day, often caused arguments leading to physical confrontations.

Alan decided that even though he would earn less being a shearer, he would have both companionship and his own time in his day to day activities and still be able to achieve his savings target. He estimated that if he could continue to obtain shearing jobs, he could possibly save seventy to eighty pounds within twelve months, after deductions for his keep and meals and frugal living. This was now his objective.

He survived his first day shearing. He did not realise the long work hours required. They started shearing at six a.m. and continued until five thirty p.m. with breaks only for lunch and morning and afternoon smokos and tea. Supper was served at six p.m.

Over dinner he met the other members of the shed team – shearers, wool classers, wool bale pressers and rouseabouts. They were a diverse group; some hardly spoke, and others just chatted about nothing, but they were not unfriendly. Some just nodded, while others shook hands, each morning greeting each other. Ten of the shearers were working under contract and the others were hired as individuals and followed the shearing season, heading south going from station to station seeking jobs.

Alan made friends with some of the non-contract shearers and they invited him to join them when they finished this shed. This suited Alan's plans as he needed plenty of work and they knew where the sheds were.

After dinner on the first day's shearing, he went to his bunk immediately and slept soundly. The next morning, he woke with tight and tender muscles in his back, legs and arms.

An old shearer saw him trying to stretch. He laughed and handed him a bottle of liniment. 'I thought you were new to the sheds. This will help a little. Rub it in and after a week you will be back to normal. But tomorrow you'll be worse.'

Alan looked at the label – *Horse Liniment*. Should he try it?

The old shearer just smiled. 'It works on humans as well.'

Alan tried it and it did help – a little.

The old shearer was right! Alan's body recovered within the week. The liniment solved his problem. The other shearers commented laughingly about the smell at mealtimes, but they knew what it was. Clean clothes and a good wash, solved the problem.

He soon realised he needed to drink plenty of water to cope with his excessive perspiration.

By the end of the week, he had gradually improved his tally to seventy sheep per day. He was indeed a natural shearer.

Alan found the evenings interesting. The shearers would tell yarns, some were probably not true, but all were entertaining.

Some told of life on the road. Others told of sadness in their life. It made Alan think more of his future and more determined to succeed with his plan. He really needed his letters from Mavis to help keep him focused.

He was worried about how to keep the revolver and the fob watch safe. It was not feasible to keep the revolver with him when shearing and he was worried that the shed humidity might damage the fob watch. Looking out of his window, he spotted a branch root hole in the tree adjacent the building. It was above ground view and was only obvious from inside his window. He decided to hide the revolver and the watch separately wrapped in greasy calico cloths in the root hole. He placed broken twigs and some dead grass over them.

Sunday was a free day. They could fish, go swimming, shoot rabbits or go for a ride over the property. Alan wrote a letter every Sunday to keep Mavis informed of his travels and his work. Often, he had to make up a few stories to fill a page. The manager took the mail and dropped it off at the Cobb and Co. office during his supplies shopping in town.

When Alan found his loneliness difficult to handle, he would seek out his shearing friends for a chat.

He was now shearing up to eighty sheep a day and hoped to achieve the magic figure of one hundred. But the station flock had been shorn and it was now pay day.

Alan's sheep tally over the five weeks had been twenty-two hundred sheep. He was paid at the rate of one pound per hundred sheep, less the cost of his meals. He had cleared eighteen pounds and seven shillings. He was delighted. He inserted his cheque into his hollow belt and collected his revolver and fob watch from the hollow tree.

After examining his horse, he saddled him, walked him around and mounted him, ready for a quick buck from him. The horse had not been ridden since before leaving Sydney. The horse was initially fractious but soon settled down and trotted around the yard obediently. Alan now dismounted and tied on his saddle bags and bed roll.

While waiting to leave with his friends he strolled over to Fred and the boss and shook hands, thanking them for the job.

The boss said, 'You have a job with *Merinda Station* any time you are in the district during shearing time.'

Alan was now recognised as a *real* shearer.

Fred asked, 'Where are you off to now?'

'My friends have told me they are heading southwest to the *Barlow Station*, some fifty miles away.'

The manager replied, 'Stay alert. A month ago, some station hands killed two aborigines they caught slaughtering sheep, and shot them. A homestead was attacked in retaliation. The tribe could be dangerous.'

The four of them rode out of the station midmorning heading into the sun. They stopped at the first inn and had a few ales and enjoyed a meal of vegetables and roast beef. The ales were enjoyable. Most stations banned grog of any description. This was the first time in five weeks he had used money from his hollow belt. His cheque would be deposited in the next Bank of New South Wales he came across in his travels.

They rode for four hours and camped by a river for the night. They intended to arrive at *Barlow Station* the next afternoon.

Alan found sleeping under the stars a wonderful experience. Laying on his back, he enjoyed the quietness of the bush and looking at the thousands of flickering stars. He achieved a peace of mind that he had not felt before.

The morning began with the kookaburras making a din, awaking the four of them. They had a dip in the fresh river water and made a typical breakfast of bacon, damper and tea.

Alan noticed smoke curling from the other bank. His first thought was – rogue aborigines. Immediately the four drew their pistols. They moved into the dense trees alongside the river and moved further upstream, away from the smoke, and crossed in the shallows.

They were correct in being cautious. Looking over the riverbank in the distance they saw a small group of aboriginal families. They were sitting by their lean to bark shelters, which he later learnt were called mia mias.

The four kept heading south west, continuing to be watchful for any armed warriors.

After about an hour they started to relax. All of a sudden, a group of six aborigines stepped out of the trees and started yelling at them. The four shearers showed their pistols but did not point them at the warriors, who surprisingly had not thrown their spears.

They just kept yelling and dancing around waving their arms but did not approach them. They seemed to be aware of the harm a bullet could cause. The shearers kept their pistols visible and Alan led them as they slowly rode past, looking directly at the warriors.

When they were safely at a distance, one of the shearers said to Alan, 'Thank God you were with us and knew what to do. That was the first time I've been in a confrontation like that. Well done.' The others all agreed that Alan had done well.

The Shearer and the Magistrate

Alan smiled, 'Well believe me or not, that was my first time as well.' They all had a good laugh at their good luck.

They reached *Barlow* early afternoon and were greeted by the station foreman, who agreed that he could use four shearers. He said the owner, George Dixon and his family, were reclusive and rarely mixed with the visiting workers. 'You probably will not see them.'

When the foreman heard of their encounter with the warriors, he shook his head in surprise. 'You were lucky. Last week they attacked our station supply wagon and injured a stockman and a horse. A warrior was shot but he ran into the bush and vanished. They are very wary of our guns and tend to avoid getting too close.'

The next morning a similar shearing day started with the boss waking the team. The *Barlow* shed was the same design as *Merinda's*.

Alan was now treated as a professional shearer. During the evening meal, several of the shearers were discussing a union to represent them. This was new ground for Alan and he wisely stood back and listened, rather than taking part in the discussion. The boss of the board was not too happy with agitators but said nothing. He wanted the shearing completed, but he remembered them for future reference.

The union issue had been building for a few years and was gaining in momentum. Only a few shearers wanted to be involved at this time, but the situation could change if wages and working conditions did not become more equitable and the work hours standard.

When pay day arrived, for four weeks work Alan had cleared sixteen pounds four shillings. He was now consistently shearing eighty sheep per day and now had cheques valued at thirty-four pounds and eleven shillings – within three months. He was delighted. Most workers had left the previous evening to visit a nearby inn. The four friends had decided to leave the following dawn.

The homestead was quiet after the shearing season had been completed. The only sounds were a few cows mooing in the distance, some owls hooting, and a piano playing a lullaby, blending with the serenity of the countryside.

Alan was woken by a loud bang around midnight. His friends all woke and when they looked towards the homestead, they could see four horses at the front of the building and one man standing with them.

Lights began flickering in the windows and voices were raised. One of his friends commented, 'I think that was a gun shot. The station may be being held up by bushrangers.'

They looked at each other. It was possible. The bushrangers may have thought all the shearing teams had left that afternoon and were unaware others were still here. None of them had collected their horses; they were still in the long paddock down by the river and unseen.

The piano started playing again and the man standing with the horses tied them up to the rail and went up the steps into the homestead.

The friends decided something needed to be done. Alan volunteered to release the tied-up horses. Using the night shadows, he managed to creep to the rail and loosen each rein. He made it back safely to their shed and they watched as the horses slowly wandered away back down the laneway.

Meanwhile another shearer went to see what was happening inside the homestead. He returned and said the owner and his wife, and two daughters were all in the main dining room together with the male cook and housemaid. They were uninjured and the older daughter was playing the piano. The four men were each sitting down, enjoying a meal. One was a very tall man, who was the apparent leader.

After his meal the tall man appeared at the front door, looked right and left and then yelled, 'Where are the bloody horses?' Two other men appeared and were immediately told. 'Well don't just stand there, go and bloody find them!' He returned and shouted at the owner. 'Are all your shearers gone?'

He replied, 'They were all paid today. Why would they stay? Their horses are gone. They must have left.'

The tall man said to no one in particular, 'I saw the station foreman and the three stockmen leave myself but if the shearing teams have gone, how did the horses get loose?' He said to Jack, the remaining bushranger, 'Take a shotgun and have a look around the sheds. Shearers are rarely armed.'

Jack headed to the stables which held six hacks, and a stallion in a separate stall. He carefully opened the main door and entered. Very little light filtered into the building. A noise in front of him made him slowly move backwards. When his back touched a cross rail he bent down and moved backwards into a stall – the stallion stall. He heard the whinny of a horse behind him. Startled he swung around and accidentally struck the stallion on the nose. The horse reared and kicked out with its forelegs, hitting Jack in the skull, stunning him. As he fell, he fired the shotgun and sent the stallion into a frenzy. The stallion mutilated Jack's body beyond recognition.

The shotgun noise startled everyone in the homestead and the shed. The owner immediately suspected the stallion's involvement but said nothing.

The two bushrangers who were sent to collect the horses had returned but had only found one, a distinctive coloured piebald. The darkness had beaten them. The tall man had found Jack and was in a quandary. He could wait until dawn and catch some station horses, but he still believed they were not alone, and he wanted to leave quickly. He decided he did not want to hang around.

While the tall man had his two men searching the sheds, he robbed the owner of money and jewellery, which included a distinctive religious cross necklace. He walked to the only horse, mounted it and rode off, deserting his men. He was lucky.

Alan and his friends were hiding in the shed with axe handles as weapons, awaiting their opportunity to attack and capture the other two gang members when they entered their shed. They struck them heavily, knocking them to the ground and disarming them.

When the two remaining bushrangers found out the tall man had fled the station and abandoned them, they swore vengeance, although they had little hope of a chance to do so, as they had committed a possible hanging offence.

George Dixon was astonished when Alan and his friends appeared at the homestead front door dragging two tied-up captured bushrangers. He punched one in the face knocking him to the ground and began kicking him. George would have killed him if he had not been dragged away. His anger had to be seen to be believed.

When everyone settled down, the two bushrangers were taken to a storeroom, tied to a wall post and locked in. Everyone then retired to sleep. It was early morning, sun-up was not far away.

At daylight, the family and the shearers had breakfast in the main dining room. What to do next was

The Shearer and the Magistrate

the topic of conversation. The shearers were leaving at noon. As far as they were concerned it was up to the owner to sort out the problem with the prisoners.

The owner made up his mind. 'They can stay locked up until the station hands return in three days and two of them can take them to town. Cook, you can feed them! I don't want to see them again. I'm afraid of what I might do.' The owner walked with them to their horses and gratefully shook their hands. He pressed a gold sovereign into each of their right palms. He realised the robbery could have been much worse for his family.

The four friends turned and waved from the top of the hill, then headed south down the dusty road. The sun was high, and the distant hills shimmered in the sunlight.

The owner had told them of a small sheep breeder who had a farm called *Woden* some two days ride away, wanting to hire a small shearing team. Woden only ran a thousand head, but they were quality merinos with large and heavy fleeces.

They ambled along. The scenery was rather monotonous; dry, dusty with only stunted scattered brush. Kangaroos, emus, and the occasional dingo, appeared in the distance. They passed dry dams and crossed two creek beds, not once seeing water. At times, Alan almost fell off his horse dozing off.

Halfway through the second day, they arrived at a small town and stopped for a meal and an ale. It was a typical town, a few shops, an inn, and a combined farrier and coach stop. A few people nodded but most just continued what they were doing and did not look up.

While enjoying his cool ale, Alan saw a saddled riderless horse wander down the street. It stopped at a nearby horse trough and started drinking. Alan recognised it as the tall man's piebald horse and walked over to examine it. It had a six-inch gash in its rump which was still bleeding and attracting plenty of flies. The horse was agitated by them. The farrier wandered over and asked Alan if it was his horse and suggested applying axle grease to the wound to keep the flies away. He got hold of the reins and led the restless horse to a stall and then smeared axle grease over the wound. The horse immediately settled down and started eating from the feed box.

The friends told the story of the robbery at the station and that the horse had been ridden by the leader. When the saddle and bags were removed, the stolen jewellery including the distinctive religious cross, were discovered in a calico bag – but no money!

What happened after the tall bushranger left the station? The farrier said the aborigines in the district were unpredictable. There had also been a few hold ups. Another thought was that he may have had an accident; an injury or an illness could have overcome him.

The farrier knew the owner of the station and pointed out where the station's foreman was sitting. Alan turned and recognised him and walked over to him. He sat down and repeated the robbery story to him and then handed him the jewellery. The foreman laughed. 'Well the boss will be pleased. If you don't want it, I'll take the horse as well. The bushranger won't need it wherever he is.'

Alan and his friends didn't want the horse. It was branded and neither of the friends wanted to be in possession of a possible stolen horse, particularly a standout piebald. Stealing horses was a capital crime.

The foreman was unconcerned. The brand was unknown in this district and he would use it only on the station.

The mystery of the fate of the tall man was never solved but many considered he had fallen foul to some aborigine rogue warriors and had been ambushed by them and killed then left to perish where he fell. Native animals would have soon attacked his remains and quickly removed any evidence of his previous existence. The colony could be harsh and unforgiving due to the many perils facing unwary wayfarers – good or bad!

The friends reached *Woden Station* the next day. From a hill, they looked down on the station and were surprised to see a large dam alongside several buildings in the middle of a barren plain. The dam water was from an underground bore. It was palatable for the animals, but it needed boiling for humans but with tea and sugar it was pleasant to drink.

Other than the shearers, there were two rouseabouts, a bale presser, his assistant and a wool classer. The owner, Edmund Kelly, showed them the shed and their sleeping quarters, also advising them his station cook would be cooking their meals.

At dinner that evening the owner introduced everyone and said he expected the shearing to be completed – sheep shorn, wool classed and baled – within five days. They all agreed it was realistic even with the heavy fleeced merinos. The shearers would be paid three pounds each with free board. A thousand sheep were ready in the paddock alongside the shearing shed and the shearing would start at sun-up the next day.

Edmund Kelly walked into the shed ringing a bell. Within half an hour the sleeping quarters were empty, and the owner locked the door.

Within five minutes of entering the shed the first sheep fleeces were ready for the rouseabouts.

The days went smoothly with the same carefree mood as other sheds. However, when two of the shearers discovered their possessions had been interfered with and each had two sovereigns missing, the mood in the shed changed.

Edmund was furious and spoke with each person separately. One of the rouseabouts became upset and argumentative, while the other one was overly cool and collected. Their attitude made the owner suspicious. He had hired them on the recommendation of the local farrier and his foreman had collected them from town. He had hired them on trust with no prior knowledge of them.

Edmund realised Alan was spokesman for the shearers and he called him to one side. He and Alan decided to lay a trap. They needed a unique item or two. Alan volunteered his initialled fob watch and the owner offered a small quality ebony pocketknife. The next day the two items were placed in Alan's travel bedroll with an insignificant piece of paper protruding an inch. A pencil line marked the inch protruding. Alan checked the bedroll for the next three days. The paper was still in position.

The shearing finished on the fifth day just before noon. The cook provided a farewell meal.

After the meal, Alan decided to change into clean clothes and went to his bed. He found that the tell-tale paper had been moved. He quietly advised the owner that the fob watch and the knife had been removed from the bedroll. After lunch Edmund Kelly paid the workers. He paid the rouseabouts last.

Alan and Edmund were prepared and had two horses already saddled. They watched the rouseabouts climb into the cart ready to be driven back to town by the foreman. After the cart had travelled about two hundred yards, they mounted their horses and rode after them.

Edmund carried a shot gun and told the foreman to halt. Then he ordered the rouseabouts to get down with their possessions. They both protested.

Edmund handed the shotgun to the foreman saying, 'Shoot them if they run.' He ordered the rouseabouts to open their bedrolls and contents. They were both very nervous but did as they were ordered. The items were not found. Their clothing was searched and still nothing was found.

Could they be wrong? Alan walked to the cart and climbed into the back-seat area. He reached under the seat and down the side panel. Reaching down he located a cloth. He dragged it out, and lo and behold, upon opening it, he found the fob watch and knife. Smiling he held it up for all to see.

The normally cool rouseabout immediately collapsed to the ground and started blaming his partner, who promptly started punching him. They let the thieves continue to belt each other until one fell semi-conscious.

The two rouseabouts admitted they stole the four sovereigns, the knife and watch. The smaller one had climbed in through an air shutter to commit the robberies before going to work.

As the nearest constable was over seventy miles away, the thieves were subjected to bush justice. The two thieves had their heads shaved, stripped then showered in green sheep brand dye. The final punishment was worse. They were turned out from the station with enough food and water to walk back to town, a two- or three-day walk. One could only imagine the reception the wayward rouseabouts would receive when they walked down the town's main street.

After they sent the rouseabouts on their way a blue-black dog came limping towards them. He stopped and looked up at them as they rode by. Alan dismounted and half-filled his hat with water. The dog drank his fill, sat down alongside him and looked up gratefully. When Alan examined his paws, he found a small sharp stone wedged between the toes of his offside front paw. It was easily removed and fortunately the paw was not inflamed.

Alan had always liked dogs and thought, *Why don't I keep him!* He would enjoy the company. The dog appeared to be a cross bred of Scottish collie, dingo and kelpie types. One of the shearers previously had a similar looking dog and praised the cross bred as being a faithful and excellent sheep dog.

He lifted the dog to his saddle and, after he mounted, he placed him on his lap. The dog needed a name. He thought of his days in England. A neighbour had a hound called Rover. Alan smiled; he was a rover as well. That would be his name. After an hour or so the dog became restless and jumped down and started running around but generally followed his horse. Alan had been concerned he would head back north, the direction he had been heading when they found him, but no! he had become Alan's dog and was duly fitted with a collar.

They kept heading due south through the dry dusty countryside. The wind created gusty, swirling dust loaded air clouds. It entered their mouth, teeth and nostrils. At times they tied wetted handkerchiefs over their faces.

The owner of *Woden* had mentioned that a droving job could be going at *Sunset,* a station a day's ride due south. As they were ultimately heading to Sydney, this job would suit them. Noon next day, several buildings appeared through the dust – a homestead, five smaller sheds and a very large animal shed. Fencing dotted the landscape separating horses, cattle and flocks of sheep.

As they approached the homestead, several dogs ran to them and started barking. So did Rover, but no dog fights eventuated, only a few sniffs. Two men walked over, nodding to them. They introduced themselves as the owner, Geoff Smith, and his son, John.

After a few general comments, they invited them into the homestead for tea and scones. They accepted the offer but, first, they requested the opportunity to wash the dust from their faces, arms and pat the dust from their clothes. The son laughed, saying he could see why; their faces were coated in dust.

Geoff's wife was a cheery Irish woman and soon had the table laid and tea set, complete with hot scones with plum jam.

Initially the talk was just chit chat seeking general news from each other. Alan raised the subject of droving. He related the advice from the owner of *Woden* and said they were heading south and were interested in the droving job.

Geoff nodded in agreement. He had been looking for a droving team to move a hundred breeding ewes to the sale yards in Bathurst for their monthly market. It was estimated the drove would take five to six days and each drover would be paid five pounds on delivery. They were to be well paid due to the night shepherding required.

The sheep could be ready within two days. John would accompany them as he had a wool press to deliver. John had established a business manufacturing them and was well known by sheep owners, for the build quality of his presses.

Geoff led them to the large shed where the ewes selected were already penned in groups of ten. He wanted their hoofs checked to see that they were not overly long and to have any necessary crutching carried out before they departed.

Alan could see they were healthy, clean and well fleeced. They looked to be quality sheep, and probably expensive. They would need to be carefully monitored.

Rover had followed them into the shed and stood quietly by Alan, looking at the sheep. Alan looked at his dog and hesitantly commanded, 'Sit!' They all smiled when he did. They had not considered if he had been trained or not. Rover would soon show his value in a droving team.

The two days at *Sunset* went quickly with the shearers occupied with the crutching and branding of the hundred sheep. A four-wheel wagon was prepared. The axles were greased, harness checked, and three horses selected.

The day arrived. The new unassembled wool press parts had been loaded onto the two-horse wagon. Food and water supplies were added to the load plus a spare wagon wheel. A spare horse was tied to the wagon tail gate.

The pens were opened, and the sheep coaxed out into daylight. John had two well trained sheep dogs and they kept them bunched. Rover was barking and running around being a nuisance. John moved down the track first, with Alan and the others moving the sheep following him. He stood up in the wagon and waved to his mother and father.

The summer weather was overcast, dry and hot. John, as the leader, told them they would travel in four hourly shifts with an hour break for lunch. Time for a break, a meal, feed the horses and to check the animals, particularly the horses' hoofs. The sheep would graze at the end of the day. The track was a mixture of tufts of grass and barren soil with no small stones to lodge under the horses' shoes and cause problems.

They made good distance on the first two days. There was ample grass and the few water holes they located still contained water, although they had been muddied by visiting cattle.

Alan did not like the night riding. But it was easy, just riding around the flock. The sheep settled down and were no trouble, but it was lonely. The more he thought of Mavis as he rode in the still country air, the more eager he became to visit Sydney. He would look up at the stars and then to the distant land. It made him feel insignificant and very lonely. Fortunately, they only rode at night for three hours each. During the day, the night riders could take turns having a sleep in the wagon – if the road wasn't too rough.

One night, Alan had a scare. The dogs started barking loudly and the sheep awoke and became restless. His first thought was – dingos.

John was now awake and saddled his horse. The others followed him with the dogs. After riding for about five minutes, they saw nothing and returned to the camp. In the meantime, Alan had managed to settle the restless sheep. John said they did not see any dingos but guessed the dogs had frightened them away. They all stayed awake that night. It made for a very long day.

The sheep walked steadily at the same pace hour after hour and the miles soon added up. John estimated that they would arrive at Bathurst around noon on the sixth day. Rover ran with John's dogs and began to help in moving the stragglers forward and keep the sides tight.

Alan normally rode behind the flock and lately began pointing to the left or the right and then say, 'Go!' He was pleased to see Rover run in the indicated direction. His dog had become an asset to the droving team.

The thick green tree lined river appeared at midday. John trotted his cart horses forward of the flock to look for a safe crossing. The river was wide and flowing slowly at its widest point. John halted the cart, hobbled the horses and walked to the bank. The water was clear and the sandy bed looked firm. John slowly started wading towards the other bank feeling for the riverbed and judging the depth. When he reached the middle, he was pleased to see that the depth was only up to his knees. He continued to the far bank and then returned, satisfied that the flock could cross safely. The alpine snows had yet to melt, hence the low water. The riverbanks showed the high marks made when the snow melted and the water poured down from up stream. His father's timing had been correct; the drovers were a few weeks early for the flood waters.

The flock were moved at a faster speed as they approached the river. They were not to stop and drink. They could drink after crossing the river. With whips cracking, dogs barking and the men shouting, the sheep were forced into the water in a tight flock. The leading sheep were moved faster than the main body, this encouraged the other sheep to follow. Within ten minutes all the sheep had crossed without loss. The cart was brought over last and it became bogged midstream. They then began unloading the heavy panels of the wool press. This work cost them several hours so that night they camped on the southern bank ready for an early start.

During the evening meal, John told them of a station owner who had erected a bridge across a popular river ford bordering his property. It was used by passing travellers including drovers. He decided to charge them a toll and, in three months, he recovered the cost of the bridge. After being legally challenged by the local mayor, he stopped charging other users. He wasn't too concerned; he had built a bridge at no cost to him.

The last days to Bathurst were normal workdays and nights – hot, dry and dusty, accompanied by boredom.

They arrived as predicted with the flock intact. Only one was lost early in the drove after breaking a leg. It was shot and butchered for food. The horses and dogs were sound. The team had enjoyed the drove but were happy it was over.

The town was a district service centre, and with the livestock sale due in two days, the streets were crowded. John had travelled ahead to arrange pens and to carry out any administrative requirements regarding ownership transfer of the flock. There were horses, cattle and sheep by the hundreds and thousands. Even cattle or sheep dogs were available for auction.

That evening the team met for a farewell dinner and to be paid. John paid for the meal and drinks. He said his father would be pleased with the number of sheep delivered. He had expected to lose ten or so and this was his way of thanking them.

That night he bid them farewell and wished them well for the future. The next morning, he and his dogs headed out of town to deliver his wool press. A quick wave and he soon vanished down the tree-lined road.

Alan had now accrued forty-two pounds and one sovereign. This, together with Mavis's money and their joint bank account, brought the balance to forty eight pounds plus seven sovereigns – over halfway to their objective! Alan had enjoyed the company of his three friends but now was the time to part. The three friends were continuing south following the shearing work.

Would they meet again? Alan would miss them and their support. He was now on his own. He was really, when he realised Rover had vanished!

Alan had not seen him for several hours after John had left town. He rode around town several times but to no avail. At sunset, with a heavy heart, he stopped at the pens of the delivered sheep, unsaddled his horse, laid a ground sheet and fell into a disturbed sleep, disappointed and angry. He presumed that Rover had followed John's dogs and would become one of his droving team. Towards sun-up, tossing and turning, he flung out an arm and struck something. He rolled over, opened his eyes and stared into Rover's face, inches from him.

He was sitting looking at him with his tail wagging as usual. A wave of delight swept over Alan as he hugged his lost dog. Today would be a good one.

During Alan's ride around town looking for Rover, he had spotted a sign advertising for a coach builder for three weeks work. Perhaps he could pick up a few more pounds. He walked into the workshop and approached a rather harassed man who appeared to be the owner. Alan told him he was interested in a job for two or three weeks and asked what it would pay.

The man was the owner, Edgar Jones, 'With board and keep, I'll pay four pounds a week, if you can finish the three four-wheel carts and a gig in that time. There they are in the corner. Market time is always the busiest for me. Have a look at them and tell me if you can do it. These two carts are owned by the mayor and the innkeeper and the gig is owned by a friend of mine.'

He continued, 'The battered old cart doesn't belong to anyone. The local constable brought it in a month ago. He found it dumped on a side road and said I could have it. If you think it's worth doing up, do it. If not, I'll chop it up for firewood.'

Alan had a quick look and could see that the work needed to be done to the first three carts was time consuming and required a professional coach builder. The old cart had a sound frame and could be used, but the body panels, the seat and the floor would all need replacing. One wheel needed two spokes replaced. He would repair the wheel only and could do the other work at leisure back in Sydney. Each of the carts were weather beaten and needed painting. Alan replied. 'Pay me ten pounds and give me the old cart and I'll do the other three within the three weeks.' They shook hands – the deal was agreed.

He and Rover slept in a small building at the back of the workshop and the owner's wife brought his meals to him and a bone or two for the dog. He started work as soon as he awoke. Some required wheel spokes tightening or replacing, all needed re-upholstering, most shafts were either worn or had lose or worn bolts. One had a broken seat, and another required a new floor. He also completed the paintwork and added a few distinctive colourful lines. When he finished the first cart, Edgar was most pleased and contacted the mayor, who was delighted when he collected it and congratulated Alan, tipping him a sovereign.

He had taken the wheels requiring new or retightened spokes to the blacksmith to have the metal rims removed. Alan refitted the spokes there and then, and had the rims refitted. He painted all the wheels except his cart. He didn't want it looking improved.

The coach work continued at a rapid rate. He worked from dawn until dinner time and sometimes into the early evening. He did the paint work in the afternoon, and due to the warm weather, it dried overnight. By the tenth day, he had completed the work required to be done on the two carts and the gig.

Edgar was so pleased with the finished work he parked the vehicles out on the street in front of the workshop for passers-by to admire. Within the first two hours he had potential customers making enquires.

When Alan told Edgar he would like to be paid as he was leaving the next morning, Edgar tried to talk him into staying, but Alan was adamant he was going home to Sydney. Reluctantly he was paid his ten pounds and, after hitching up the cart and installing a temporary seat, he threw his gear, his saddle and bridle and some fodder into the back of the cart. After a quick farewell to Edgar and his wife, he and Rover headed east to Sydney.

The further east they travelled, the more the road improved. It was now normal to see more traffic – passenger coaches, both large and small, lone riders, family carts and military squads.

He was surprised to see the number of men walking west, singularly or in groups. Probably they were on their way to the gold fields. The vegetation slowly changed from the red coloured soil and stunted brush to light green grasslands and spindly trees. In the distance the mountain range separating the inland plains from the coastal flats appeared in a blue haze. It looked forbidding but obviously roads had been built for the development of the interior of the colony and were now being utilized by the populace.

Alan was advised to allow at least two weeks to reach Sydney. The roads were in reasonable condition, but the journey had many difficult hills to traverse. Rain was a major problem as it made parts of the roadway very slippery and often caused minor flooding and even small landslides. He camped out most nights, sleeping in the back of the cart. Sometimes he stayed at an inn spending a shilling or two and taking the opportunity to wash.

As they approached the mountains, the grass became greener, thick and luxuriant, and livestock became more prevalent. He stopped and looked at the foothills of the mountains. They were thick with dense shrubbery and an endless carpet of tall trees. He continued up into the hills. Sunlight became filtered and at times non-existent.

As he entered an area without trees, he became aware of dark clouds forming up ahead. He hurried the horse to a faster rate hoping to find an inn before any rain fell. The road surface was loose and showed signs of previous strong water flows washing the topsoil away. It was nearly three hours before he came to an inn. The inn appeared dry, but that was all. The innkeeper and his wife were grubby and smelled. He was the only patron. However, they cooked him a meal, accompanied by a warm cup of tea. He retrieved his bed roll from the cart, then found a corner to sleep and, with the dog by his side, he soon fell asleep.

He was awoken by a lightning flash, followed seconds later by a roll of thunder and down came the rain. It poured and poured for an hour but fortunately the inn roof did not leak, and the shutters had been closed. When the storm had passed, he opened a shutter facing the road. Alan was surprised when he saw the road was wet but not flooded and was also undamaged. The excess water was flowing down the far side of the road towards a small ravine.

The innkeeper said the road had been improved by the current governor, who had ordered the Road Works Department to install weather drainage systems to protect this important road, within six months. That was twelve months ago. The department had reworked six road sections, totalling eight miles, with drains alongside the road edges. Three bluestone bridges had been erected and several small road sections dug out. Tight fitting bluestone rocks were embedded in the road surface, allowing excess water to flow over the road, leaving a firm surface for man and beast to transit without causing any flooding or back water to build up.

The next morning after a quick wash at the horse trough and a very ordinary breakfast, Alan hitched up the horse to the wagon, loaded the gear, gave a quick wave to the innkeeper, and with a flick of the reins he and Rover headed east towards Sydney. The innkeeper had been right. The improved road showed no sign of erosion from the previous night's storm.

They crossed a few more hills during the week and gradually began to descend. In the distance he could see the countryside was changing, and they were on the coastal side of the mountain range. There were still hills to cross but, in the distance, he could see open grassland and smoke. Alan was slowly descending a long multi curling section of road when he noticed a coach and several people milling around in a road curve down below him. He stopped; it looked wrong! Suddenly he realised it was – a hold-up. There was nothing he could do but watch. It was over five minutes away and there appeared to be no violence occurring. Alan kept watching.

After a few more minutes the coachman reloaded the passengers and headed east. He counted four robbers who had now ridden off into the bush.

Alan continued down the road, carefully keeping to the middle of the road on the bends. Within half an hour he began to leave the trees. As he turned to the straight section of the road, he heard the shout, 'Bail up'. Startled, he turned to see the four robbers on the side of the road alongside the trees. He had his revolver under his shirt, but he made no move for it.

He blurted out nervously, 'It's no good robbing me; I've no money.'

The leader laughed. 'Yes, you can go. I can see by the condition of your cart you're battling. It's a wonder it hasn't fallen apart. On your way.'

His companions laughed. They turned their horses and headed back into the bush.

Alan sat there shaking. The surprise ambush had unnerved him. He flicked the reins and slowly headed east again. During the ambush the dog had been half asleep in the cart. He lay there, alert, quietly watching the event and fortunately had not reacted.

Other travellers began appearing and gave a wave and a friendly greeting. He had been on the road for nearly eleven days and more settlements now lined the roadside. Smoke hovered over a small town a day or so ride away. He mused he would soon be home and back with Mavis; only a day or so to go.

He stopped at the next inn and asked for a horse stall only. He would sleep in the cart. The weather was warm, and he enjoyed the fresh air. Most inns had an unpleasant smell either from the kitchen, the owner, the staff and/or the unwashed patrons. After feeding the animals, he took the saddle from the cart and laid it between the stalls. He sat down and started eating some cheese and sliced dried meat.

A commotion erupted in the inn. Alan looked around and saw a police sergeant motion him to be quiet and stay where he was. He and two other constables lined up alongside the rear door of the inn. They were armed with two double barrelled shot guns and the sergeant had two revolvers. A gun shot sounded in the inn and out rushed two men.

The sergeant called, 'Surrender in the Queen's name.' The men paused and then started to run. The police immediately opened fire with the shotguns. The men fell dead without uttering a sound.

Another man ran out with two pistols raised and was shot by the sergeant. One pistol slid across the ground to the horse stall where Alan was still sitting on the saddle. He looked at the police who were peering down at the dead bushrangers. He pushed the pistol under the saddle and then stood up and walked over to the group.

The whole event was over in five minutes. He had seen a gun shooting and three men now lay dead twenty yards from him. Was he dreaming?

He looked down at the bodies. He recognised them as the bushrangers. The last slain man had been the one who had spoken to him yesterday. The fourth man had been shot inside the inn. The sergeant turned to him and explained that his squad had been told of the coach robbery and had been looking for these men. They were well known in the area. Alan told him of his encounter. The sergeant said he had been lucky; they had been a dangerous gang.

Later in the afternoon when the bodies had been moved, the sergeant walked over to Alan. 'Two of their horses are branded, but the other two aren't and neither of the bridles or saddles have names on them. So as far as I am concerned, they are unclaimed stray animals. Our pound is full of stray horses. If you like you can have one and take it off our hands. I'll give the other one to the innkeeper for arranging their burials.'

The offer surprised Alan. He nodded and walked over to check them. His horse could do with a rest after nearly two weeks of towing the cart. He selected a four-year-old bay gelding. It appeared healthy, had clear eyes, a shiny coat and was well shod. He thanked the sergeant, who just shrugged his shoulders, shook his hand and walked back to his men.

When the police left the inn, Alan retrieved the pistol from under the saddle. The owner was dead, and it would not be claimed. It was a modern Navy Colt .36 calibre six shot revolver. It fired bullets and not balls. His pistol was unreliable with the old powder and cap design. When he reached Sydney, he would purchase a shoulder holster to wear under a coat. It had been his lucky day and he celebrated that evening by enjoying a steak meal and an ale or two.

Alan had previously designed a brand – an A with an M welded to the base of the A. He took both horses to the local blacksmith next morning and had a branding iron made. Both horses were then branded with an A on top of the M.

He would register the brand when he arrived in Sydney. He decided to name the bay gelding Champ and his jet black mare, Tess.

After his daily ritual of checking the hoofs, watering and feeding the animals, he was on his way. The road was now reasonably flat but still had many twists and turns. At one stage he came upon a queue of travellers held up by the police. He was advised that a bullock team with a large log was approaching and needed nearly all this section of road due to the many tight turns.

Alan pulled to the roadside and decided to take the opportunity to rest the animals. In the distance he could hear the loud crack of a whip and a shouting voice. As he looked towards the noise, he saw the first of the bullocks appear around the nearest corner. The beasts were in twos and were plodding, plodding and plodding along with a continuous and monotonous rhythm. He watched idly and began to count the bullocks. When they totalled eighteen, the log started to appear.

The log was large and long – approximately five feet in diameter and thirty feet in length mounted on a sub frame. Alan was amazed. The number of bullocks was impressive, the log size was impressive but the wheels on the sub frame were most impressive. They were made of solid hard wood. The axle holes had been formed with hot irons burning through the wood. The wheels were about four feet in diameter with the centre over one foot thick then tapering to a rim of ten inches. As a coach builder he could only shake his head at this ingenuity. He realised this heavy load would have needed exceptionally strong wheels. They were the biggest and strongest wheels he had seen.

The picture was completed with a tall slim bushman swinging a whip around his head and then flicking it to generate a loud crack. He supplemented the crack with a few choice words to encourage his bullock team.

He called the leading bullocks by individual names. Alan wondered if he had a name for each of the eighteen. The whip handle was six feet long with a lash eight feet in length. The bullock driver handled it as if it was a gig whip. Accompanying him were two other riders and a cart loaded with hay.

The traffic built up over the three-hour wait took an hour to clear. It was almost dark before he moved out and was on the road again.

The remainder of the trip was uneventful after the bushranger saga. He soon arrived in the outer Sydney area. Houses and shops began to be a normal sight. After spending so much time in the sparsely occupied western district, it was a welcome change of scenery.

The difference between the poor and the rich citizens was most apparent. Their dress, means of transport and many with just a superior air, deserved or not, contrasted with the posture of those wearing dirty and dishevelled attire, walking with heads bowed.

Alan stopped at a general store to buy a typical

Australian present for the family. An opal pendant for Mavis, a rural picture for his parents and a local pottery vase for Uncle John and Aunt Anne.

As he left the shop, he saw a man walk towards a horse, mount and ride off. He had a limp. No, it couldn't be!

It was Sean Kennedy. The tide had carried him ashore to the entrance to Corio Bay, a small bay to the west of the entrance to Port Phillip Bay. He was found by a local farmer and had survived to cause more trouble. He had joined a ship in Geelong and sailed to Sydney.

Alan planned to arrive home just before dinner and, right on time, he stopped the horse in front of the stables and workshop. It was still daylight; the doors were open. Alan unharnessed the cart horse and put both horses in stalls.

Alan opened the rear door, climbed the stairs and walked into the dining room.

John saw him first. 'Hail the wandering hero returns! Welcome home.'

They all turned and rose as one to greet him home. His mother started crying with delight. Mavis put her arms around him and kissed him, without saying a word.

Alan's hands were shaken by both his father and his uncle. After a minute or so they all sat down, Alan sitting close alongside Mavis. They agreed to ask about Alan's journey after dinner and to tell him now what was happening in Sydney.

After dinner they sat in the armchairs and relaxed with a drink or two as Alan related his travels. He spoke for nearly two hours before he stopped and distributed his presents. His family looked at him with pride and the men with envy.

Later, alone with Mavis, he told her of the money he had saved. When he told her they had accrued sxty-six pounds, she went to a drawer and, smiling, handed him ten pounds. 'This is my contribution.' A total of seventy-six pounds. They were well on their way to their target of one hundred pounds.

They sat up late into the night discussing their future. Mavis agreed when Alan said he would work his way to the Murray River on the Victorian border and further south, maybe even Melbourne. He had read that land was available in several districts for either purchase or lease. They both agreed they wanted to be farmers and work their own country property. A timeframe of three months was agreed. Within that time, he hoped to increase their savings to around one hundred pounds and identify a property or land to lease or purchase. The next day they told the family of their plans. The family received the news with mixed feelings but without objection.

Alan towed the cart into the workshop, accompanied by John's laughter and started removing the side panels and the seat. John thought it was waste of time trying to repair it but he soon changed his mind when the cheap wood used for the panels and seat were removed and revealed that the main frame and seat box were made of hard wood and were in good condition. Within the week Alan had replaced the side panels and made a new seat with a quality padded leather cover. After his experience with the rough roads to Sydney, Alan decided to fit some leather strap suspension between the main frame and the axles. It was a simple design. Several wide leather straps were shackled tightly between the frame cross members and attached under the axles. Spare straps were stowed in the seat box.

He repaired the wheels as necessary, fitted a spare wheel under the floor and painted the entire body a dull green. The cart had a lack lustre, cheap and ordinary appearance but it was what Alan wanted for his travels.

When refitting the seat, he had trouble opening the seat box as it was nailed closed; he had ignored it before. With a lever he managed to open it.

Old clothes, some general tools, two small bags sewn tightly at the top and an old shotgun were its only contents. Alan put the contents under a bench top and then washed and painted the inside of the seat box. The metal attachments did not need replacing. They were worn but still in reasonable condition. The final task was to fit a weather cover to the side panels of the rear box section. John had a large canvas sail covering some timber at the back of the workshop. Alan cut out an excess section of canvas to fit between the four sides and nailed one side to the back of the seat panel and made eyelets alongside the other three sides of the canvas. The other three side panels had nails hammered part way to hook onto the eyelets. The cart rebuild was now complete.

Mavis and Alan often walked around the local streets during the daylight hours. Night-time was risky with the rogues and vagabonds roaming free. They were making up for the months they had been separated and spoke of their future and how they would achieve it. During their strolls Alan purchased a shoulder holster and two boxes of bullets. Mavis said nothing but guessed why he needed them. She had not forgotten his stories of his adventures of the past months.

Neither looked forward to the coming lonely months but they had their dream and intended to pursue it. He had been home for a month and was now ready to depart. After a family farewell meal, Alan left early the following morning, loading the saddle and bridle together with his sleeping blankets and clothing. He placed the old shotgun and pistol in the seat box. They were old and still fired but were unreliable in a crisis.

His trade tools, his coach building manual and a shovel etc. were also loaded. A few kisses, hugs, and Alan was gone, driving the cart with Champ harnessed, Tess tied to the tailgate and Rover, panting and barking, happy to be sitting alongside his master.

CHAPTER FOUR

The Partnership

Alan drove down past the shops through the small village and by midmorning he had reached the main road. A battered and tilted sign pointed to the south west – Goulburn 120 miles – Gundagai 130 miles – Melbourne 550 miles. The accuracy was doubtful? Alan was on his way and was not overly concerned at the mileage.

He had planned the trip to take about twenty days travel time and hopefully average twenty-five miles per day with rests at Goulburn, Gundagai, Albury and Euroa. He would seek work for a few weeks at a time and use the other time to look for land or a property to lease or purchase and then move to another shearing shed. He had spoken to previous travellers who agreed it was a realistic and achievable objective.

The road headed south west. It was wide and the surface packed down by the many cattle herds and sheep flocks that had trampled on it for the last thirty odd years supplementing the herds and flocks in the colonies of South Australia, Victoria and the New South Wales southern and western districts. Water was a problem in the summer months, as indeed were bush fires. Droving teams always had experienced bush men with them just to travel forward to identify water locations and tracks for them.

The road surface was reasonable and the surrounding countryside green and dotted with farms and livestock. The scene was worthy of a painting by a quality English landscape artist. Several times coaches raced rapidly past him in either direction. Horsemen were not uncommon and gave a wave when galloping, making puffs of dust. Small hamlets or settlements appeared around every twenty or so miles, the distance many travellers preferred for their horses and to stop overnight.

Alan parked the cart near a general store or an inn whenever he stopped overnight. After he wrapped a blanket around him, he pulled the canvas cover over. He felt safe with Rover and his revolver in his shoulder holster.

The first week he made good time and stayed a day in Goulburn at an inn. Unfortunately, he did not get any jobs between Sydney and Goulburn, but he still had a long way to travel.

Two days from Gundagai, Alan could see a large dust cloud in the distance. Within two more days he caught up with a large herd of cattle spread out so far that the cart couldn't get pass them.

A stockman rode up, apologised and advised the herd would be at the Murrumbidgee River at Gundagai town the next day and they would be using the east crossing. He said there was a smaller crossing to the west that would suit Alan. The stockman advised him after he left town, he should take the narrower left track as only sheep flocks travelled along it and the sheep were easily parted and he could pass through them.

Alan thanked him and kept close to the herd, ready to move to the west when the river appeared. It was a very imposing river. From a hill he could see Gundagai to the east and the cattle moving in that direction.

He spotted a narrow section of river behind the town and headed the cart towards it. He was right. He crossed the river and was now in front of the cattle herd. From the top of the hill he looked back towards the herd and could see the cattle bunched up at the river crossing and the stockmen cracking whips and shouting, forcing them to keep moving. He guessed it would take them the rest of the day.

Alan continued until he reached the next town. This became their rest day. The next day, fortunately, the first inn he stopped at he found a farmer who had need of a shearer.

He followed him for mile out of town to a picturesque farm overlooking the magnificent river. Below the farm, he could see the river flat extending far into the distance. The farmer saw him looking and told him of the time two years ago when the river flooded, and the water was five miles across. Three months after the waters receded the entire area was lush green grass. He fattened over two thousand sheep on it for six months and made a packet of money. He turned and asked Alan to follow him.

The owner had over a thousand sheep to crutch. It was necessary for the health of the sheep to keep the anus area clean to prevent fly strike. Flystrike in sheep in a large flock was generally fatal for the sheep as it could go undetected in large flocks.

His son had already moved the flock into the home paddock. Alan was asked to help the owner's son drove the flock into the shearing shed pens the next day and be ready to start crutching the following day. The owner had allowed five days for the crutching and he offered Alan five pounds for the crutching time and the day he had assisted his son. They shook hands on the agreement.

The son moved the sheep into the centre race for Alan to drag them out. Shearing the sheep was easy and quick; it was the catching and dragging the sheep out that was time consuming. The two worked efficiently and averaged two hundred per day and emptied the pens in the planned five days. The son swept the board and filled a bale with the crutchings. It was exhausting work and Alan slept well each night. He stayed another day and, after being paid, he loaded the wagon. He hitched Champ to the wagon, tied Tess's halter to the tailgate, had Rover jump aboard, a quick wave and away they went, heading south. He had enjoyed the seven days he spent there.

Alan had left Sydney over fifteen days ago and had covered over two hundred and eighty miles but had only made five pounds. Still he had a long way to go to reach the Victorian border and plenty of time to earn more money.

The next planned rest town was Albury, a major farming centre on the Murray River. Four days travel had Alan at the entrance to a large sheep station. He could see that the shearing shed was a hive of activity, with sheep in the holding paddocks.

Alan rode down a track leading to the shed and hailed the man standing on the landing, 'Do you have any jobs for a shearer or coach builder?'

The man laughed and said, 'Climb down and let's talk.' After introductions he learnt he was talking with Ian Jones, the station manager.

Ian told him he only had around one more week of shearing, but he could give him two or three more weeks repairing the station's horse drawn carriages. During high winds the barn roof had collapsed and damaged most of them. Alan agreed.

Ian said, 'Come and look at the damage. You can work as a shearer until we finish the shed and then stay on and repair the vehicles.'

The barn roof had not been completely removed but he could see the damage to some of the carriages was substantial and he definitely had a few weeks' work. He asked Ian what was the going wage.

He replied, 'Three pounds ten shillings and keep per week.' They shook hands and Ian took him to the sleeping quarters. 'I'll see you in the shed tomorrow.'

The day dawned with noisy birds, shouting men and general noise. He followed the other men into the shed and waited until the manager pointed him to a vacant stand.

All of a sudden, the clicking of shears started, accompanied by bleating of sheep and the shed became alive. The manager walked up and down checking the shorn sheep for cuts. The tar boy was nearby ready to cover any bleeding cuts to protect sheep from the dreaded fly strike.

The shearing was completed on time as expected. Alan then concentrated on the carriages. The roof had been supported by a beam extending between the two barn end walls. Only the northeast wall had a large opening in it. During the storm the barn doors were closed, and Alan surmised that an extreme gust had filled the barn and lifted the roof up and moved it from being aligned with the beam. The roof panels then came down on the support pylons which penetrated them and down came the remainder of the roof. The coach in the middle of the barn was the most damaged. Its top and the seats were crushed, and it had two wheels with snapped spokes. The two work wagons were solid and only two wheels had been broken. The gig was the least damaged, only the seat and the left shaft damaged.

The shed had not been repaired. The first job was to remove the broken roof panels. Ian had two general hands assist Alan to clear the debris from the barn. The roof panels were awkward but the three of them managed to drag them out with the help of a horse. It took over three days to repair the panels. They would be refitted later. The biggest job was to place the beam back into position. One end had dropped down when a wall swayed outward in the wind. They managed to lift the beam by hoisting it higher than the top of the wall, with a jury-rig, and then lowering it back into its original position. Within five days the roof panels were back in position and the barn was now reusable as a workshop.

Alan decided to repair the gig first. The shaft had cracked lengthwise but had not separated. He pinned it with nails and wound thin wire tightly around the repair for a length of ten inches. It would not break in the repaired area again. He repaired the seat by replacing the broken back plank with a packing case side he found in the barn and reusing the upholstery from the broken seat section. The two work wagons' wheels needed five new spokes. He found several small hardwood trees and set about cutting them to shape. The station had a small forge. His two helpers were also put to work firing the forge. Alan heated the metal rims until they expanded and could be hammered from the wooden wheel.

Shaping and shaving the spokes took two days of sawing, rasping and hardening over a fire. After fitting the new spokes, the rim was reheated and hammered into position. A coat of paint, some axle grease and the two wagons were ready for work. Three carriages finished, one to go! The coach would take some effort and thinking. The station had little to assist in the way of materials. He would have to improvise.

First, he dismantled the top of the coach and then the seats to decide exactly what he would need to complete the repair. The two wheels would be repaired last. The three top iron frames were bent, and one had cracked a bolt hole. Alan straightened the frames and drilled new holes each side, equidistant from the ends on the damaged frame. The ceiling material had only a small one inch cut, and he sewed the ends together. The packing case provided two suitable seat planks, and after refitting the upholstery, the seat was as good as new, well almost. He painted the inside and the outside of the coach with black paint, including the wheels. He was surprised to see how smart it looked and mused how much better it would appear with two matching horses in black harnesses trotting down a capital city road.

Alan had almost lost track of time. He sat down and started to tally the days – six shearing, five dismantling and rebuilding the barn, one on the gig, three days re-spoking the wheels for the wagons. The coach had taken six days. He had worked a total of twenty-one days and had been at the station twenty-four days. The time had passed quickly, and he had enjoyed the work. But it was time to be on the road again.

Ian had been away for two weeks and had not seen the work that had been carried out. The carriages were all in the barn when he returned. Alan was at the barn door and waved.

Ian rode up with a smile on his face, admiring the rebuilt barn. He said, 'It looks as good as it was before the storm.' He then asked, 'Have you finished the carriages?'

Alan nodded and opened the barn door. He could see Ian was delighted as he walked around, inspecting them. Pointing to the wagons he commented that the loose spokes had been tightened and then said the coach now looked like new. The owner would be pleased.

Ian paid him fourteen pounds. 'Any time you want a job, just drop by. You can always have one here.' A handshake, a wave and Alan was heading for Albury. He had accumulated nineteen pounds so far.

Both horses were overweight, and he allowed them to set their own pace for the next days. Rover did his own thing.

Alan kept to the parallel track of the main track as the drover had advised him and found the surface in reasonably good condition. The district comprised long rolling hills with grasslands and scattered forests. Some areas were settled with buildings visible in the far distance and livestock grazing. Mobs of kangaroos would bound along and he saw a few emus feeding in the open grasslands. Stockmen and stagecoaches passed by more often the further south he travelled. He felt less lonely when he returned their waves and greetings.

A call of 'Hello' made Alan turn and he saw a rider approaching, waving.

He rode a magnificent black gelding and sat as if he were riding to the hounds. Well dressed and clean shaven, he asked, 'Are you heading my way?'

Alan asked, 'Which way would that be? I'm travelling to Albury.'

The newcomer introduced himself as Godfrey Armitage. 'My home is just over the next hill. I thought we could travel together.'

Alan replied, 'I'm working my way south and am looking for work.'

Godfrey replied, 'Well, if you want work, we can give you some.'

Alan smiled, 'Join me and show me the way.' They chatted and headed towards the hill.

Godfrey explained he was a remittance man who had become involved with a daughter of a local laird. She had become pregnant to him, and the laird was going to kill him, so his father, the Earl of Montany, had ordered him to leave England immediately and not to return in the laird's lifetime. Godfrey had moved to Australia and was now living with his brother and his family at this station, while being paid a remittance by his father.

The station homestead was built of bluestone and surrounded by several different sized wooden sheds. A few large paddocks were fenced and had horses and milking cows. A large flock of sheep were on the horizon. Several forests with tall green trees were scattered over the large open countryside. The sheds were a collection of large barns, a shearing shed and sleeping quarters. Each building had a water tank. A large lagoon was about a mile from the settlement with a creek running by it. When the creek flooded it topped up the deep lagoon.

Godfrey introduced Alan to his brother, Owen, and Owen's wife, Alice. Their children were in Sydney at school. They were a happy couple and welcomed him as if he was a long-time friend. They led a lonely life.

They sat on the veranda, talking and enjoying the traditional tea and scones as they exchanged news and talked farming. Owen needed a general hand for a week or so checking the fencing and carrying out any required repairs. Alan agreed and Godfrey showed him to his sleeping quarters.

The next morning Godfrey met him and escorted him to the breakfast room and explained the layout of the station. He had loaded the work wagon with materials, tools and food.

They headed out at noon; Alan driving the wagon and Godfrey riding his horse. They would camp out as needed by the workload and as determined by the weather.

The fences consisted of poles inserted into dug holes then wooden planks were inserted horizontally into three slotted holes in the poles. The poles were prone to movement after heavy rain and cattle rubbing their rumps on the planks. The fence was firm and straight for the first mile or two but afterwards the fence line bent and some planks had come lose from the poles. The work was monotonous, but between the two of them, they made good progress and rammed the loose soil down at the base of the poles and straightened the fencing. The planks were easily replaced after cutting them to their correct length. The old planks were loaded on the wagon to be used as firewood at the homestead.

Sleeping out at night was a delight. The skies were clear, no wind and it was warm. Godfrey was good company. Naturally he was well educated and had a few years in overseas military service in India. Surprisingly he was a competent manual worker and could swing a mean axe. They lay on their bed rolls and swapped stories, at peace with the world. Rover had come with them and slept by Alan's side.

The fencing continued for four days and they headed homeward when the food was running out. Once they shot a kangaroo for fresh meat and had a feast, with a few choice steaks and boiled potatoes. Water was plentiful from a nearby dam, and they had a swim, accompanied by Rover. Even the horses were led into the shallows and washed. They were home in a day. Owen was happy with their report that his major fences were in good condition. He paid Alan four pounds. They then enjoyed a few beers, sat around and chatted about the future of the colony. Alan decided to leave at the weekend, in two days.

The Shearer and the Magistrate

The next morning Alan awoke with a throbbing head from too much homemade beer and a thudding sound from outside his window. He staggered out of bed, dressed and went to the horse trough for a wet towelling to freshen up. The thudding sound was being made by Godfrey looking fit and healthy, punching a suspended half full chaff bag hanging from a tree.

When he saw Alan watching, he stopped. 'This is my favourite exercise and I have neglected it for too long. I'm trying to recover from last night's over imbibing. You should try it sometime. I competed in fist fights at home.'

Alan had seen many fights in shearing camps, and some had become very violent. He had kept to himself.

Godfrey had raised the issue of boxing several times in the past week, wanting Alan to learn. The following morning, he watched as Godfrey strapped and taped his hands. He thought, *Why not give it a go. We're friends so it should not get out of hand.*

He had his hands bound. They faced each other as Godfrey explained the technique on how to throw punches. They spared slowly at first and gradually began to make contact. Godfrey mainly threw his punches straight from the shoulder and Alan had a swinging action. They gradually began to make firmer contact. Godfrey hit Alan hard on the nose and it began to bleed.

He overreacted, when Godfrey threw the next left-hand punch. Alan brushed it aside and stepped in close punching him hard in the solar plexus. A whoosh of air escaped Godfrey. As he bent forward, Alan instinctively punched him in the jaw. Immediately he went to Godfrey, who had gone down on his hands and knees, gasping for air. He sat alongside him as he recovered his breath.

Smiling, Godfrey looked up. 'I must remember that combination. It's effective. Let's call it a day and go have a drink.' They walked back, side by side, still friends.

The last evening at dinner Owen asked where he was headed. Alan told them he was looking for land or a property to lease or hire, probably in Victoria. Godfrey told him the northern country was rugged with several rivers, a mountain range, few formed roads and mainly only tracks. Owen handed him some month-old Victorian newspapers to read. He thought perhaps they might help him in his search. Alan read them from the first word to the last word, until late into the night.

The large central area between Seymour and Ballarat seemed the best potential district. Much of the area had been settled by squatters and was now being subdivided by the Victorian Government. This had not been received with good will by the squatters. After Owen's advice, Alan decided to leave the cart at the station and travel with the two horses; one could act as a pack horse.

The weekend arrived and after a quick farewell he was on the road again. Godfrey decided to accompany Alan to the nearest town. He went to town once a month to buy food and collect his remittance cheque from the coach office mail room.

They stopped at a roadside inn for a meal and an ale. This was when he saw Godfrey's fists in action and realised that even though he had beaten him a few days ago, he would be no match for him in a real fight.

Two drinkers took exception to his posh accent and kept annoying him. Eventually he invited the two to go outside. He shaped up – in the classic stance. They laughed and at once they both attacked him.

He hit the first one with a vicious punch to his throat, turned to the next and stepped to one side, punching him in the jaw. Both had been knocked down and were left moaning in the stable yard.

Alan shook his head, laughing. 'You didn't need me.'

They then continued their meal. Alan said he planned to return to the station within the month. They then headed to the coach office for their mail and the general store. They shook hands; Godfrey headed home and Alan headed south to the next town.

Alan was leaning against the hotel veranda post with a beer in one hand and a letter in the other. It was the first mail he had received from Mavis in over a month. They had now known each other for over a year, and he was looking forward to marrying her. He had nearly saved enough money to either purchase or lease a country property or land.

He mused he had been away, mainly shearing, a little droving, coach building and fencing work, for too long, but the letters from Mavis helped him tolerate the loneliness. It was around two months since he had seen her and his family. He missed her, his parents and life in Sydney town. He had accrued twenty-three pounds so far this trip and intended heading home within the next month or so, after he had identified a property or land.

A loud crash made Alan turn towards the hotel door. Two wrestling drunks staggered out through the door into the street and continued fighting. The bigger man knocked the other down who fell to the ground. He lay there moaning for a few moments then rolled over and promptly went to sleep in the street. His assailant then wandered down to the riverbank and went to sleep on the grass. The hotel patrons continued drinking, ignoring the drunks. It was a typical pub scene expected in the rough and raw colonial country lifestyle.

The district had several large sheep properties and now that the shearing had been completed, many of the shearers were now 'lambing down'. 'Lambing down' consisted of shearers going to the nearest hotel, then handing over their pay cheques to the publican and drinking until they had no more credit. Not all shearers went binge drinking; Alan was one of them.

He enjoyed a beer but was focused on saving for his future. Whenever possible he even slept outdoors under a shade cloth, except when shearing when he used the sheep station bunk house.

The local constable, Ed Miles, was a typical tough no nonsense individual. He was a product of the 'Old Dart' and had immigrated to the colony two years ago. He was respected and had the support of the locals. During the 'lambing down' periods his small three jail cells were nearly always full – up to twenty drunks were housed in the cells until he judged they could leave.

They weren't always fined. Some were made to clean the jail, the police stables and sweep High Street. Others were even made to whitewash the two government buildings. It helped to keep the town nice and neat and meant less paperwork for him. Belligerent drunks were often given physical help out of town. A black eye or thick lip was not uncommon after a confrontation with Ed.

The hotel was the only one in the small pioneer town on the Murray River with a population of around five hundred. In only a few years it had become a district centre for the collection of local wool, grain, timber and for the distribution of general trade goods for the farming community. Several well stocked stores, together with the government buildings lined High Street on one side and on the other side was a blacksmith, a farrier and several general trade services.

At weekends the population doubled with visiting farm workers collecting their weekly supplies and having a leisurely drink and a yarn with their mates in town. Their women would congregate at the Country Woman's Association Hall to catch up on the local gossip and enjoy a cuppa.

The river was, not only a popular fishing place, it also had a small pier which was ideal for loading wool bales and timber onto the new paddle steamers servicing the towns up and down the important river. Surprisingly the town area offered employment for nearly one hundred people. The local shire contributed by hiring a dozen or so men on road works maintenance. It was a typical colonial country town, friendly and welcoming.

CHAPTER FIVE

Testing Times

Alan needed to move on. He wanted to begin searching central Victoria for his dream as soon as possible. He inspected the two horses, saddled up and headed south. He had been advised the next town was only two hours' ride. As he reached a rise overlooking the main buildings, he saw a scuffle outside a hotel. A shot rang out and a man fell to the ground. At first, he thought it was a robbery, but he then realised that he was seeing a smartly dressed man being bundled into a two-horse cart and covered with a blanket. It had the appearance of a kidnapping. The cart accompanied by two horsemen then travelled quickly out of town. Alan watched as they headed south into the trees and shortly afterwards reappeared, turning to the west into further trees. The crowd was still standing around talking and had made no move to chase them.

Alan rode down to the group and asked what happened. A young man explained that the visiting magistrate had been kidnapped by the Marsh gang, a notorious family of ruffians. A rider shouted as he rode north that he was going to tell the police. Alan took Tess to the stables and asked the blacksmith to look after his horse for a few days.

Alan headed out of town in the direction he had last seen the Marsh gang. He was surprised at the lack of action by the townspeople. Little did he know the reputation of the gang or the unpopularity of the magistrate's court hearing's potential decision.

Within an hour he had sighted the gang and continued to follow them at a distance.

They kept travelling until sundown when they arrived and stopped at a small farmhouse in a clearing. Alan headed back towards town in the moonlight. He met a party of riders lead by Constable Miles and flagged them down. He related his story and astounded the riders when he said he knew where the gang was hiding. Some didn't believe him as he was a stranger, but Miles remembered him and advised he had brought along a black tracker who could help prove Alan's claim. Four riders agreed to accompany the constable, Alan and the black tracker to free the magistrate. The constable had informed his superiors by mail via Cobb and Co.

The four riders and the tracker each had rifles while the constable and Alan had six shot revolvers. Each rider had a bedroll, water but no food. They rested overnight and arrived at the small farm midmorning. After the tracker did a surveillance of the property, he advised that they had left a few hours ago. The fireplace was still warm, and they were heading west. He found the cart had been left behind and there were now four horsemen. Constable Miles sent a horseman back to wait at his office and to update his superiors.

The black tracker travelled several hundred yards in front of the others and found their tracks easily.

Obviously, they were not expecting to be tracked so soon or not at all. Late afternoon the tracker came back and said they had camped about two miles down the road in a small clearing.

Constable Miles said, 'We need to plan how to rush them in the early morning. But first we need to know exactly where the magistrate is positioned.' He asked the black tracker to check the layout of the land and note where everyone was, in particular the magistrate.

The land was flat with two trees opposite each other on the fringes of the clearing. The magistrate was tied to one tree and the four horses were on a longline tied to the other tree. The gang were camped in the centre of the clearing around a campfire. It was decided to attack at first light. Alan was to go protect the magistrate and get as close to his tree as possible before first light. The constable and the others were to concentrate on the gang only and be careful not to spook their horses.

They took turns having a few hours' sleep. Before sun-up they began making their way into their positions. The constable and the others followed the black tracker through the trees and scrub.

Alan worked his way around to the other side of the clearing and eventually got to within twenty feet of the magistrate and waited, his heart pounding with anticipated excitement.

The constable stepped out into the clearing and levelled his revolver. He shouted, 'Surrender in the Queen's name' and fired his revolver into the air.

Alan ran to the magistrate. 'You're safe now.' The magistrate just sat there as Alan untied his arms and legs.

One gang member tried to raise his pistol and was immediately shot in the shoulder. The other two surrendered and raised their arms. It was all over in

The Shearer and the Magistrate

a matter of minutes. The gang member with the bullet wound was helped up onto a horse and tied on. The other gang members were handcuffed, and their feet tied to the stirrups.

Alan noticed that the heavily bearded one of them had a limp and was vaguely familiar, but he was more interested in supporting the magistrate who had introduced himself as James Newton.

Constable Miles and the others hurriedly headed off to town with the three prisoners. They were the district heroes for weeks and enjoyed many deserved free ales.

Alan and James leisurely rode back, slowly recovering from the dramatic climax to the attempted kidnap. Richard had been taken to Melbourne and was recovering in hospital.

James explained the reason he was in this district was due to a case concerning the sharing of the water rights of the Murray River with farmers whose properties were bordering either side of the river. The river was the border between the two colonies but the river was in the Colony of New South Wales. The case was difficult – a legal no win situation. James had decided to take the matter back to the Victorian Government for them to sort out at the next Intercolonial meeting.

The Marshes were unhappy with him after he gaoled their young brother resulting in their hair brained idea to kidnap him. They were going to ask the Victorian Government to exchange him for James. Two of the kidnappers were brothers but one of them was not. He was an Irishman; that's all he knew of him. Alan had a vague feeling that he had seen the bearded Irishman before.

Over dinner that evening at the local inn, the two new friends relaxed over a few ales and discussed their past lives and what they were seeking for their future.

When Alan started talking about his dream of becoming a landholder and breeding sheep, James began to show an interest and started to ask questions. He told Alan that, although he wished to pursue a legal career, he also had a vision of being a country landowner.

James thought for a moment and then suggested, 'Why not a partnership? I have some money and you have the expertise.' Alan listened and nodded and suggested that they both sleep on it and discuss the idea next morning at breakfast.

Next morning Alan told James he liked the idea and told him he could contribute a hundred pounds. He asked James, 'You're a legal man. How would the partnership work?'

James said, 'Simple. We would form a company. I would put up two thirds of the money; you would manage the farm and we would share the profits or losses.'

Alan nodded. 'Let's finish breakfast and then sit down and do some forward planning.'

James was heading south west to his next and last country court hearing. This was the area Alan had planned to check out. Naturally they travelled together. They had set a cash limit of one hundred fifty pounds and this was a realistic price for the local land offered at auction and two hundred for a property with a good dwelling and shedding. More possibly with stock. They preferred a purchase rather than an auction.

There was an auction at the first town where James's court case was being held. They both attended to get a feel for the auction process.

Twenty blocks were offered and were all sold within an hour. Alan was surprised that few bid against each other once the figure reached around two thirds of the final figure, which was almost the same for each block.

James smiled. 'I can see you are wondering what's going on. It's a ploy called 'Dumming' used by squatters to have 'Dummys' bid on their behalf to increase their land holdings. They acquire the block and then work it for the squatters. They make it difficult for a new farmer to purchase blocks adjoining the larger holdings.'

The two friends rode across country to James's next court hearing. The land varied from open grassed plains to thick forests with water plentiful in lagoons and creeks. Smoke appeared in a clump of trees in the direction they were heading. The grass was lush and green with part of it fenced alongside a creek with a small flock of sheep.

A border collie came barking towards them followed by a tall lean middle-aged man with a shot gun under one arm. He motioned them to stop. 'Who are you and what do you want?'

James and Alan dismounted and shook his hand, introducing themselves as travellers. The man looked at them, sizing them up. He nodded to them to follow him to a dilapidated shack. The inside was crude and basic. The hut was a large bark shed built in an open section of the surrounding forest. A log fence of saplings and posts with y-sections had been erected around it to give a semblance of order to the scene.

He had cultivated an area and was growing potatoes and some root vegetables and a few fruit trees. They all looked healthy. A fowl run was totally enclosed with coop wire with a lift up hatch to access eggs. Two horses and two cows were in another enclosure with a basic cow-bail. Two lean-tos were attached to the hut. One accommodated a small plough and a horse harness. It was a farm but very limited in output.

He opened the hut door and gestured them to enter. The kitchen consisted of homemade furniture. Saplings hammered into the ground supported a bark tabletop with the side seats made the same way. A bed was a suspended canvas hammock with a straw mattress. He was apparently an educated man; a collection of study manuals and notebooks were on a wooden food box. The fireplace had a grill and a water boiler suspended over the fire area. Several boxes three feet high were along one wall with clean clothes hanging neatly above on nails. A gun rack had a rifle stowed and two hooks with a saddle and a bridle. The floor was a mixture of soil and animal dung pounded hard. It was not an unpleasant smell. One wall had farming tools with odds and ends stacked along it. The far wall had aboriginal artefacts hanging from a beam – spears, woomeras, shields, clubs, coolamon dishes, possum skins and a few not identifiable.

He introduced himself as Jonathon Irons, Faculty of the University of Manchester – Department of Anthropology. He had come to Victoria to study the aborigines and their culture. He apologised for his surroundings but said he did not want to show any affluence to them. He felt it would discourage them from meeting him. He had achieved only limited local success and was considering moving to Queensland in the immediate future. He had little interest in the farm; he just operated it to survive.

When James and Alan told him who they were, Jonathon said, 'I could see by the way you were dressed and spoke that you were respectable. I need to be on my guard around here. I've had a few scares. I think the local squatter is behind them.'

Alan commented, 'You have selected good land in a good position with water. It's a pity you're not a farmer who could stay and develop it. If it was closer to Melbourne, we could have been interested in purchasing it.' James nodded agreement.

Jonathon replied, 'Yes, I know it's good land. The squatter has his eye on it and I'm sure he will move in the moment I leave. He can have it all for a few pounds. I need to be back in university in twelve months with my thesis and I need to obtain much more data. My time is running out.'

James interrupted. 'We must go. I have some court cases in two days, and we have quite a few more miles to cover by night fall.' They walked to their horses and wished Jonathon success in his venture and rode west.

The ride was easy. Country tracks became more obvious with a few farms and livestock appearing on the horizon. They stopped at a small village for a cooked meal and directions and found they were on course and, more importantly, on time. They only had a half day to travel to arrive late afternoon.

The courthouse had an inn next door. After organising accommodation, James went to the noticeboard to check the listed hearings. His first hearing was scheduled for tomorrow at noon with two more hearings the next day.

After James had completed his country magistrate duties he returned to Melbourne. Alan decided to be based in the town and continue to search central Victoria in a circle.

After nearly two weeks he had not identified any suitable properties and began to become despondent, wondering if he should give up and return home.

When he returned after a fruitless search, he found an excited James waiting. He had been waiting for him for a day. He was all smiles. 'I think I've located a farm two days ride south. He's a friend of a friend and wants to return to England. And he wants a quick cash sale. I've a few days free. Are you ready to come and look right now?'

Within the hour the friends were on their way south. Alan's mood changed quickly; he was now excited.

They rode until it was dark and unrolled the sleeping blankets, fed the animals, lit a fire and then had a basic meal followed by a mug or two of tea and an early night. They slept until the kookaburras woke them with their raucous call.

James had a hand drawn map showing a large rock formation to the east of the property with a river on the north boundary. After travelling up a few wrong tracks, they ended up on a road looking over a valley. Nestled in a clump of trees, they could see a bluestone building, a small single room cottage and a few wooden sheds. Several hedge fences enclosed a few paddocks by the river. Sheep and two cows grazed near the farmhouse.

James said, 'We're here.' Alan was pleased and nodded.

They rode down a long track looking left and right at the condition of the paddocks as they approached the farmhouse. The grass was lush and deep green and the animals looked in excellent condition. A woman opened the front door and waited for them to dismount and walk to her.

A friendly voice said, 'Hello, and who might you be?'

James spoke, 'I'm James Newman. We have a mutual friend who said that your property might be for sale. I hope that is still the case.'

'Yes, that's correct. Please come in and meet my husband, William. He's doing some paperwork. I'm Jenny Forbes.'

A tall solid man entered, smiling and they shook hands. 'Please be seated.' His wife left to prepare tea.

'Yes, you are correct. We must return to England urgently. Our only son was badly injured in a horse fall and will need constant care for many years. We have several other properties which he was managing in England. My wife is returning to England next week. I will follow as soon as I have settled my business in Victoria. I am seeking a reasonable offer in cash. The property is ours, free and clear. It consists of the farmhouse, a farm hand cottage, a barn, some shedding, farm equipment, a four-wheel cart and heavy duty dray, two hundred acres consisting of four paddocks, together with three hundred sheep, one cow with an unweaned calf and two horses. I'm seeking around three hundred pounds.'

His wife served tea and cakes. James and Alan had tea and excused themselves to talk privately about the price. They debated the figure and decided to offer two hundred and thirty pounds first with a limit of two hundred and sixty pounds. The livestock warranted offering a higher price.

James said, 'I am a magistrate from Melbourne and unfortunately the farm is not close to a town. However, we are prepared to offer two hundred and thirty pounds and payment within two days.'

William said nothing for a few moments. 'Make another offer and I'll consider it. I can appreciate the problem of distance. I travel frequently myself.'

After delaying a few seconds James nodded. 'Two hundred and fifty pounds is our limit.'

William put out his hand. 'Agreed.'

James handed over twenty pounds as a deposit. Alan was surprised he had that much money on him. The friends had bought their farm. They arranged to meet in the Melbourne Bank of New South Wales at noon in two days. James would return to Melbourne and settle the purchase and draft their business agreement.

Alan asked if they could call the farm *Woodlea* after his grandfather's farm in England.

James agreed. 'Yes, we can call the company the same name.' Alan would stay in the cottage until James returned. He would write and ask Mavis to come to

Melbourne with the money as soon as possible. He told James he would ask her to come to his Melbourne address.

Jenny was in tears. Her husband was going home with her to their son. They immediately started packing.

They invited Alan to dinner that night and told him why they had come to Victoria. Jenny had been unwell for a few years and it was recommended that she have some time in a warmer climate. They had only come for six months but when a friend decided to move to Melbourne and offered them the farm at a good price, they decided to stay indefinitely. Jenny loved the views.

She was an accomplished artist and had continued to paint when they moved to the farm. She had completed ten paintings of the local country landscapes and wildlife. She had already packed them ready to ship to London for sale. She showed Alan an unfinished painting of the riverbank with birds featured. She was very good.

William was writing his family history and lecturing on finance at the Melbourne University. They had been content with their lives until the news of their son arrived.

Alan found the cottage cosy with some basic furniture. He strolled around the fence line critically inspecting the posts and cross poles. The river was shallow and clean; fish were visible. The two sheds were solid, built with poles, planks and bark panels. The larger one was a barn for the carriages. At one end were two horse stalls with a saddle, harnesses and bridles and halters hanging on pegs. The other building was a small shearing shed. It had two holding pens, one to supply sheep to the shearer and the other, a holding pen to do the branding and drenching. It was a simple layout but effective. A table in the middle was the fleece working bench and there were four shearing stands. The cow had a milking bail in a lean-to alongside the barn. The farmhouse was a three-room bluestone building – two small rooms, one a bedroom and the other a general room. These joined a larger room which served as a dining and kitchen area. The furniture was sparse but of reasonable quality. Alan was impressed with their purchase.

He sat by the river and wondered what Mavis would think. The farmhouse was small, but a larger room could be attached on the dining room end. Apart from that extra cost, he believed the paddocks could support more sheep. That night he wrote a long letter to Mavis explaining how events had unfolded, giving her the news. He explained why he had agreed to purchase the property without having time to consult with her and hoped she trusted his judgement. He finished the letter, requesting her to come to Melbourne, bringing the money. She could stay here for a while and then both of them could return to Sydney to marry. He included James's Melbourne office address for her to contact on arrival.

William and Jenny soon completed packing their baggage and luggage, ready to return to England. Early the following morning Alan drove them and their goods to Melbourne. They left their goods with the shipping company and then went to the Melbourne Club to stay until their ship sailed.

They were to meet James at noon the next day. Alan had lunch with them, bid them goodbye and bon voyage and headed to his new home, after delivering Mavis's letter to the Intercolonial Coach Office.

Fortunately, it was a full moon. He arrived at the farm in darkness after nearly making a few wrong turns. He had tied Rover to the cow bail, and he began barking when he heard Alan approaching. He had been left food and water, but the dog was pleased to be released, jumping and running in circles in delight. Alan now had four horses, too many perhaps.

While waiting for James to return, Alan drafted a building design to extend the bluestone building. He planned to add another room onto the end of the dining kitchen room. A room forty-five feet long with an eight foot ceiling. He would remove the dining room wall and relocate it to the new room far end. A new interior wooden wall would replace the removed bluestone wall. The general-purpose room would serve as another bedroom.

Alan fed the animals, inspected the horses, the cow and calf. He drove a few sheep into a small pen and inspected their fleece and body mass. They were all in excellent condition.

The sheep would need crutching in a few months and shearing in eight to nine months. He considered riding around to the local farms, offering his shearing service to earn some money.

He and James needed to do some forward planning. They would need to earn money and inject it into the farm to make it a viable proposition. The going price for wool was twenty-one pence per pound – a sheep averaged three pounds of wool, skin three pence each and tallow for candles was seven and a half pence per pound. Alan was planning an income on these figures. Shearing would be another source of income. James's income was predictable as he was on a salary. They needed money in the company account.

They had a next-door neighbour a mile or so away. Alan decided to meet with him and say hello. He was greeted by a rugged ex-sea captain, Alistair Crisps, who invited him to share a whisky or two with him. They chatted in general about their lives and plans for their farms. Alan headed home when he became a bit wobbly from the whisky but remembered to invite Alistair to visit him.

James arrived on time at the bank to be greeted by the Forbes'. A bank clerk was sitting with them enjoying tea. James handed over his credentials and the money transaction was quite simple. The Forbes' had their lawyer waiting at another table. He expedited the transfer of property ownership documents into the company name, *Woodlea Company*, and handed them over to James.

They were now official property owners. He went back to his office to collect the Partnership Agreement for him and Alan to sign. It was time to head north to the farm.

He was pleased that everything had worked out so easily. As he rode towards the farmhouse, Rover bounded to him, barking and jumping. Alan looked out of the barn door and waved. They shook hands, happy with achieving their objective.

They sat down and James told him of the payment and transfer of the title into their company name. He also laid out the Partnership Agreement for them to agree. They would go to town tomorrow to have the Partnership Agreement signed and witnessed.

That night they say down to plan what they considered could be done in the future, and how. They discussed the extension, Alan taking on some local shearing and upgrading the flock to merinos. Alan suggested they look around for some casual help. After a short discussion they agreed. Mavis's anticipated arrival was of concern. James was required to be in Melbourne for the next two weeks. Hopefully she would arrive within this time. In anticipation, James took a cart with him to Melbourne to carry back her luggage to the farm.

Ten days later, at noon, Richard knocked on his door and escorted a young lady into the office. 'A Miss Mavis McDonald to see you, sir. I have stored her luggage downstairs.'

James came from behind his desk. 'Thank you, Richard. Hello, Mavis. I've been expecting you. I'm James. How was your journey?'

Mavis took his hand. 'Long and tiring but interesting. It's a big country.'

'I suggest that I check you into a hotel to rest tonight and we will head to the farm tomorrow morning. First, let's have lunch and get to know each other. Alan will be pleased that you are now here. He misses you.' James opened the door and escorted her to the hotel next door. He settled her at a dining table and then went to book her room.

Lunch was comfortable. James found her to be a relaxed, confident woman and could see why Alan had been attracted to her. They both spoke of their families and their interests. Lunch did not last long. James could see she was tired and encouraged her to go to her room and rest. He suggested that she have dinner in her room. They agreed to meet at eight a.m. and drive out of Melbourne to the farm.

The morning was sunny with no wind. Mavis was refreshed and greeted James enthusiastically, looking forward to seeing her new home.

Their horse trotted through the suburbs of Melbourne for an hour or so. Then small green fields began to appear, dotted with livestock. The sky was clear, and the clean smell of fresh air became apparent.

The Shearer and the Magistrate

After living in Sydney Town, Mavis noticed this most obvious improvement.

Around noon they were nearing the farm and when they reached the top of a small hill, James reigned in the horse and turned to Mavis and pointed. 'There's your new home.'

Mavis just stared, not saying a word. James was shocked and thought that she didn't like the property. After a few seconds she turned and smiled. 'It's beautiful.'

Alan was tightening the hinge on a shed door when he saw the cart approaching. His heart started pounding. She was here at long last. He waved and he could see Mavis excitedly waving back and James smiling at their happiness. They hugged and kissed unashamedly. James discretely took the cart to the barn and unharnessed the horse.

After Alan showed her to her room, they walked around the property as he proudly pointed out the buildings and their contents. They ended up sitting by the river watching Rover paddling in the shallows.

Mavis said, 'I knew you would buy a good property. This is unbelievable. Our next step in our dream is to get married. Can we go to Sydney soon? We've been apart too long.'

Alan nodded. 'I was going to talk to you about that. I'm ready to go as soon as possible. We'll discuss it with James tonight. I don't want to leave the farm without someone here. Perhaps our next-door neighbour can keep his eye on it.'

Dinner that evening was a happy event, helped by a wine or two.

Mavis suddenly stood up. 'I have a surprise for you.'

She went to her bedroom and returned with two small calico bags. After laying a cloth on the table she emptied the bags of small whitish rocks. The men gasped in astonishment – they were looking at gold quartz.

Mavis continued, 'John found them under the workshop bench. He saw you put them there when you were working on the cart in the workshop.' Alan thought for a second or so and then remembered the bags and the shotgun hidden under the seat panel.

Alan explained, 'I was given an abandoned cart by the police as part payment for a job I did and I repaired the cart in Sydney. It took a few weeks' work; it was a wreck. These bags and an old shotgun were under the screwed seat panel. I forgot about these bags. I wonder what this gold is worth. I'm sure it will help pay for the extension.' The three were delighted with their good fortune.

James said, 'I have to return to Melbourne tomorrow. The government assayer is across from the courthouse. I could get his opinion on the value. You would get a better price from them.'

Alan replied, 'If he will buy the gold, sell it. We can use the money. I'm not interested having it sitting in a bank.' Mavis nodded agreement.

After James reported to his office, he told Richard he would return within the hour. The assayer office clerk took the bags, weighed the contents and then ushered him into a side room. He knocked on a door, entered and within a minute returned with the government assayer, a tall unsmiling man. An introduction was followed by a critical examination of the quartz.

He asked, 'Where did the gold come from?' He always asked this question, as he was required by law.

James replied, 'Central New South Wales.' This was where Alan received the cart.

The assayer said, 'I will require evidence to support your statement.' This request was a waste of time as he knew most statements of gold finds were false.

'I am a Melbourne magistrate. My word should be good enough.'

The assayer looked at the clerk who nodded affirmation. He had seen James in court. The assayer asked James to return at noon for the valuation.

At noon James entered the assayer's office and was shown to the side room. The assayer had some paperwork in front of him. He was smiling. 'Even though it is in quartz, there is a good quantity of gold. I have valued it at one hundred and twenty-five pounds. If you wish to sell the gold, I can arrange cash for you now.' James kept a straight face, even though he wanted to jump for joy. He nodded in agreement.

After he returned to his office, he collected his mail and checked his in-tray. He had two reports to complete and three hearings to prepare for, due within a fortnight. As each task could be done at the farm, he decided to head there next morning. He wanted to tell Alan and Mavis as soon as possible. He wanted to see the expressions on their faces when he gave them the good news.

Richard said he would let him know if anything urgent arose. He watched James ride out of town.

The trip was boring, but the weather was pleasant, sunny and there was no wind. He trotted the horse to the front door and found the two of them waiting in anticipation.

They sat down, poured tea and he looked at James. He pulled out a roll of five pound notes and put them on the table. Mavis started to count them – first twenty, then forty, sixty, eighty, one hundred, and finally, one hundred and twenty-five pounds.

The tea had gone cold. Alan spoke first. 'Well, we definitely have enough money for the extension, to hire a farm hand and return to Sydney to marry.'

As per their long-term plans, Alan and James had been considering having a farm hand, particularly when he and James might both be away.

One day when shopping for supplies in Ellensvale, the local town, he read the local church noticeboard and saw a notice –

>   Retired Soldier – Pensioner.
>   Seeking accommodation.
>   In return for farm work.
>   References.
>   Contact Joseph Hall c/- Rectory.

Alan knocked on the Rectory door and a polite and well-spoken man greeted him. 'Good day. Can I help you? The minister is away for the next hour or so. I'm Joseph Hall.'

'I'm Alan Chadwick of . I read your notice looking for accommodation. I am looking for a farmhand who will work for accommodation and perhaps a small wage at a later date. Can you tell me some of your background?' asked Alan.

After Joseph collected his references, they strolled around the rectory gardens and Joseph started to talk. 'I originally hail from a Lancashire farm and joined the British Army when I was twenty years of age. I spent thirty years in the Corps of Engineers and retired as a sergeant major before immigrating to Victoria six months ago. I saw action many times and came here to forget. I am not married. All I want is a quiet life, and I do not drink. Financially, I have a small but adequate pension.'

Alan read his references and handed them back, nodding his acknowledgement. 'Can you come to my farm tomorrow so we can talk more? Here is a map of directions.'

Rover started barking and Alan looked up as a horseman appeared, riding down the farm lane. It was Joseph Hall. He dismounted and they shook hands.

After tying up his horse, Alan showed him the property. They walked to the river, around the fences and then the buildings. When Joseph entered the small cottage, he had a look around and nodded acceptance. 'What tasks would I be required to do?'

'Mainly you would maintain the farm, equipment and fencing; help with the shearing and see the animals are healthy and fed. I intend to grow vegetables and some fruit trees. They will need to be established in time. Next month I will be starting to extend the blue stone cottage and I would want you to do that with my help. What do you think?'

Joseph replied, 'This could be what I am seeking. I can handle any task you have mentioned. Regarding the building, that will not be a problem. I'll need some practice at milking when the calf is weaned.' He looked at Alan. 'I'm happy to come on board on your terms.'

Alan said, 'Good. I'll be in town this time next week. I'll pick you up.' A handshake agreement and Joseph headed back to town, whistling.

Joseph was sitting on the front porch as Alan drove up in the cart. He loaded a gentleman's travel chest onto the cart and a long narrow box wrapped in canvas. He smiled as he saw Alan's puzzled look. 'A gift from the regiment.'

They chatted on the way back about the farm potential. When they unloaded the chest, Joseph said, 'I can see that you are curious about the box.' He unwrapped the canvas to reveal a long polished mahogany locked container. Unlocking the container, he withdraw a magnificent modern long barrelled single shot rifle. It was metallic blue with an octagonal barrel. The metal was engraved with – *Crimea – India – New Zealand – Africa* – and included small maps of the countries.

The wood was highly polished and had a bronze plate inserted – *Presented to Sergeant Major Hall for service to the British Army – Corps of Engineers – 5th Regiment.*

On the top near the breach was a small eye glass and a micro adjuster. Alan guessed that it was a sniper's rifle and wondered why he had been presented with a memento such as this, if he was an engineer.

Joseph explained, 'It's a long rifle used for sharpshooting. I competed in the army contests and won the open shot for short range targets. I treasure this gift and you are the only person in Victoria who knows I have it. I trust your discretion.'

Alan nodded. 'It might be an idea for you to hide it.'

Joseph soon settled into a routine and carried out his tasks without prompting. Daily he would dig garden patches and plant seeds, feed the horses and cows, clean the stables, and weekly, inspect the fences. He then began levelling the wall base preparing for the extension.

When the wall base was ready, he made two trips per day to collect bluestone blocks from the nearby quarry, five miles distant. The heavy-duty work dray could carry twenty-five bluestones per trip. When the cart returned to the farm the bluestones were unloaded and fitted directly into position onto the wall, saving double handling. Alan's job was to have the mortar mixture ready when Joseph returned. Slowly the extension started to take shape. When James came up for the weekend, he joined in the work. Alan had allowed two months to complete the extension.

The decision where to have the wedding was solved

by Mavis's mother. She suggested that as neither of their parents had been to Melbourne before, this would also be an opportunity for a holiday for the four of them to come down by coach.

Alan checked in town to ensure accommodation was available. The suggestion was then agreed, and the women arranged a date for the wedding and the Sydney visitors' arrival date.

The extension was ahead of the target date. The two outside walls had been erected and, with the extra money, it was agreed the interior wall would remain and they would purchase more blue stones to complete the new entry wall.

Joseph said he would design it. His drawing showed a rather ornate and impressive doorway. They all agreed with it. Within the month the extension had been completed, including a carpet covered wooden floor. They now had their farmhouse. New furniture had been purchased, including a desk for James to carry out his office work at the farm.

Alan was pleased also, because when James was home, he had been sleeping in the dining room. At least now he had the main room until the couple were married. Then he would have his own room again. James wasn't concerned as he was away quite often and he had his accommodation in Melbourne, but Alan had felt uncomfortable.

Alan had advertised around the district and had several offers to shear some small flocks of between one hundred and three hundred head.

He was only away from home a few days. Joseph came with him at times and acted as rouseabout and was paid for this work. James was away for a week at a time travelling around central Victoria. Mavis had taken on the duties of the housekeeper, performing the cooking, cleaning, washing and tending the garden. They were all busy.

Their parents arrived and were settled in the Ellensvale Inn, a cosy bluestone building owned by an Australian born couple from Sydney. They were soon swapping stories of Sydney Town from years gone by. Ellensvale was mainly a service centre for farmers with shops and outlets supplying anything from chaff to sugar and everything in between. Clothing and similar up market goods required a trip to Melbourne to the bigger stores.

The six of them decided to travel by train to Melbourne to stay for two days. Alan and Mavis left the cart at the town stables. After they checked into the London Hotel they strolled around the major streets until the women spotted a clothing store advertising wedding dresses and suits. The men declined to accompany the women. William and John went back to the hotel and Alan walked over to the courthouse to say hello to James.

James was busy in a hearing court. As Alan started to walk to the hotel, he noticed a person walking towards him, stop and look at him. The stranger quickly turned and went to a horse, mounted it quickly and rode away in the opposite direction. The stranger had a limp and even with the beard, Alan suddenly realised he had seen Sean Kennedy again. It all came back to him. He was certain it was the same person he had seen at the attempted kidnapping.

Alan immediately went to Police Headquarters and asked for the duty inspector. Ryan Dodson, a veteran from Dublin invited him to a side office. 'What can I do for you?'

When Alan explained that he had seen the 'Wanted for murder – Irish Assassin – Sean Kennedy', Inspector Dodson became interested. He asked a clerk to check the Ireland files for a Sean Kennedy. She returned with a small folio. The first page was a charcoal portrait drawing of Kennedy.

Alan said, 'It is a very good likeness, although he's clean shaven. The eyes, forehead and head shape are recognisable.' The inspector then read the attached reports.

The inspector said, 'Our clerk is a very good artist and I would like you to sit alongside her while she draws some pictures of Kennedy with various beards. It may take some time, but it is important.'

Alan agreed. She was quick and good. They had the bearded version within the hour. The inspector thanked Alan and promised to keep him informed of any developments. Alan told him he could leave any mail c/- James Newton – Melbourne Courthouse.

When Alan arrived back at the hotel after talking with Inspector Dodson, the others had already dined and were having drinks in the lounge. He sat down and looked at his father. 'You will not believe me, but I have just seen the notorious Sean Kennedy two streets from here.'

The others sat there wondering what he was talking about. William then told them the story of the assassination of the Mayor of Waterford a few years ago and that Sean had gone to school with Alan. Kennedy had escaped, presumably as a stowaway on a ship and had simply vanished.

It had been a successful day for the women. They had selected dresses for the wedding and now wanted Alan and James to be fitted with their suits. Reluctantly they went with them the next morning to be measured, prior to returning to Ellensvale on the afternoon train, while James returned to court. They would return next week for a final fitting. The train travellers were glad to leave the smell of Melbourne's polluted air for clean country air.

The following week Inspector Dodson was required to attend the Monday morning briefings of the previous week's events of interest. One event involved the escape of an Irishman with a limp. He had escaped from a prison van taking him to hospital. He had told the prison authorities he had previously had rabies and had it again and said he was unable to walk.

His cell mate told the authorities he had been making soap flakes and putting it in his tea and was blowing little bubbles as a foam. The authorities had panicked and sent him in a wagon, unshackled.

On a long bumpy road, aided by the noisy banging of the axle springs and the wheels thumping, he had kicked the wagon door open, jumped out and vanished into the dense bush. His escape was not discovered until the wagon arrived at the hospital.

Inspector Dodson decided to visit the prison to show the drawing to the two guards on the wagon and the Irishman's cell mate.

His suspicion was correct. The three each agreed that the drawing was of the Irishman – Sean Kennedy. Alan Chadwick *had* seen the wanted man. What to do now was the question?

Out of the corner of his eye something attracted Joseph's attention as he was riding, inspecting the fences. Turning around, about three hundred yards away, he saw the sheep running and spreading out in all directions. Two large dogs had dragged down a sheep and were killing it.

He had heard of wild dogs and their habit of random

killings and realised he could have a problem on his hands. James was away and the others had gone to Melbourne by train, shopping for the wedding dresses and Alan's suit. He sat on the horse for a while, thinking of what to do.

He soon decided and rode quickly to the farmhouse, dismounted and hobbled his horse. He went inside, unpacked his rifle, collected four bullets and walked to a small rise overlooking the paddock. He lay down, unfolded the two front legs and adjusted the micro eyesight.

One dog was still tearing at the carcass, the other was standing looking towards Joseph. Joseph aimed at that dog's chest and fired. The dog just dropped dead. The other dog looked up at the sound of the explosion. Joseph calmly reloaded his rifle and fired at its chest; it dropped dead.

Joseph walked back to the farmhouse and left the rifle there. He untied his horse and rode down to the dead sheep and dogs. The dogs were big mongrels. He wondered to whom they had belonged but without any real interest.

He tied the dogs' rear legs together and slung them over the rump of the horse, rode down to the river and threw them in. The water was fast flowing, and the dead dogs soon vanished downstream, slowly sinking from sight. He collected the dead sheep and removed the skin. He laid it on a bull ants' nest behind the barn, it would be clean by morning and after washing and greasing it, he would use it as a floor mat. He carved meat cuts from the carcass that would to be fed to Rover. The carcass remains ended up in the river. He cleaned his rifle and returned it to the box and hid it away and then he washed his horse down. As far as Joseph was concerned that was the end of the matter.

He did not intend to tell anyone of the incident unless specifically asked.

Several weeks later the captain dropped by for a chat and happened to mention that his nephew had been visiting and his two dogs had run away. The captain said they were no loss. They had been viscous dogs and he was glad they were gone. Joseph just nodded and said nothing.

The wedding day was fast approaching and another trip to Melbourne was required to finalise the clothes fittings and collection. The families looked forward to the train trip. They only intended to be in town for a few hours and return in the late afternoon. The women had prepared a hamper and a flask of tea to enjoy midway through the journey.

Alan had a window seat and sat looking at the distant mountains. The countryside paddocks were a verdant green with very few dry areas. Forests leading up to the ranges were dense all the way to the top. They reminded him of a carpet.

Alan had travelled to the ranges peak once and it took all day dodging through the trees and scrub. The wildlife was impressive. He had seen countless noisy and colourful birds, wombats, wallabies, echidnas and, when having a drink from a creek, briefly he spotted a platypus coming up for air before it vanished below the water. He had felt like he was alone in a different world.

With the train frequently blowing its whistle near road crossings, they reached the suburbs with steam pouring from the engine. Young children waved to them.

The families chatted away, talking about what they intended to do today after their clothes were successfully fitted.

The women went to their preferred shops while the men went to a livestock auction to pass the time. They were purely onlookers. Alan and James had enough horses and sheep, but they were interested in the current selling prices.

They all met at the railway station, the women carrying the clothes and their new purchases. The train had only one carriage with very few passengers and departed on time. It was scheduled to arrive at Ellensvale at nine p.m.

The trip up into the ranges was uneventful, but as it was halfway up the long climb, the train slowly lost speed and finally stopped. The engine driver came into the carriage and advised that the steam regulator had split open and he was unable to develop a sufficient head of steam for the pistons to turn the wheels. They were stranded in the ranges – a known bushranger hideout. For once Alan was unarmed.

He looked around the carriage at the other passengers. They were an assorted group. Four men sitting at the front looked capable of handling themselves. The next row down were two elderly women and their husbands. He guessed they were farmers.

A family with three children, three young men and Alan's group comprised the remainder of the passengers.

The engine fireman came into the carriage and said he could see a farmhouse on a ridge a few miles away and volunteered to walk to it and get a message to Melbourne. He would fire two gunshots to let everyone know when he reached the farm.

The engine driver said, 'We'll be alright, but it might be a very long wait before help arrives.' Within an hour two shots broke the quietness of the ranges.

The four men started to talk among themselves. One, who appeared to be the leader, stood up. 'We're members of the local Volunteer Rifles and have arms in our kitbags. We will organise a roster to ensure we have two men acting as guards throughout our wait, so relax and stay calm. Yes, it is a known outlaw district, but we will change into our uniforms and go on duty.' Within ten minutes the mood had changed from one of concern to one of comfort.

The engine driver brought a large container of hot water into the carriage. When a farmer's wife saw the hot water, she pulled out a large packet of tea leaves and offered it around.

The hot tea was appreciated by everyone and when someone else produced some biscuits, the occasion became a light supper.

The night was cold and there was a full moon. However, the patrolling footsteps of the riflemen crunching on the ground in the stillness of the night encouraged most passengers to sleep. Couples cuddled together to keep warm.

Alan listened to the sounds of various animals echoing in the forests but had difficulty in identifying them. Some were birds, others he could only guess at.

Alan wasn't frightened but he would have felt more comfortable if he had his revolver with him. He eventually went asleep holding Mavis in his arms.

Dawn was heralded by the raucous call of the kookaburras reverberating through the treetops and soon had everyone awake. No one could sleep when a few of them really started laughing. The engine driver had kept the boiler fired all night and greeted them with hot water for tea. Some passengers went for a walk to stretch their legs, staying within view of the train and the riflemen. Eventually a rider appeared. He dismounted, and introduced himself. With a flourish he produced several loaves of bread and a jar of jam. He was from the farmhouse and reported that he had roused one of his farmhands and sent him to Melbourne as soon as the engine fireman had told him of the problem.

The passengers treated the occasion as a light breakfast in a picnic environment in the hills. Everyone was cheerful and had accepted their misfortune in good spirits. It would be a story to be repeated within their families for years to come.

A distant train whistle advised of their approaching engine. Within an hour the engine was coupled and started pushing the disabled train to its destination of Ellensvale. During the long wait, the passengers had come to know each other and became friends. As Alan and Mavis only knew a few people in Ellensvale, they decided to invite them all to their wedding, even the engine driver and the fireman. Laughingly they all accepted.

When Alan and Mavis did not return as planned, a concerned Joseph rode to town the next morning. He decided to go via the railway station first and was surprised to see a crowd gathered there. When he asked around, he was told the evening train had not arrived. He was thinking of what to do when a train whistle signalled its imminent arrival. Alan and his group were the last to disembark. That evening Alan told him the story – all's well that ends.

The wedding now gathered momentum. Alan kept out of the way and found a few days shearing to perform within a day's ride of the farm. He and Joseph made a good team. He soon learned how to handle a fleece, trim it and roll it for packing into a bale and the subsequent bale pressing. They handled two hundred sheep in three days.

The women had arranged the hall, catering and the church service. Mavis had sent out invitations and all had accepted. The guests were their fellow train passengers and local town tradesmen and shopkeepers.

John and William found small jobs to do around the farm when Alan and Joseph were shearing. The captain came over several times with a 'wee drop' and the men went down to the riverbank and told their stories. They enjoyed each other's company.

The wedding day arrived sunny, and there was a pleasant light breeze. A perfect day. Alan and James stayed in town for the previous night. Richard remained at the farm to drive the bride and bridesmaid in a borrowed coach. Joseph would drive their parents in another borrowed coach.

They all arrived at the church on time, even the bride. Typical of a small idle country town on a weekend, many locals came to the church to see the wedding. Some they had not met and may never.

Alan looked at his bride walking up the aisle. He felt pride at having Mavis agree to be his partner for life. She looked beautiful.

Mavis also had similar feelings. She was happy; she had her heart's delight and a wonderful home.

The ceremony was a whirl. It seemed to be over in a flash. One minute they were taking their vows, the next minute listening to speeches. Richard acted as Master of Ceremonies and showed his auditory skills. No doubt his court experience helped him. After the meals and toasts, the band started, and the newlyweds performed the bridal waltz. The celebrations continued as Alan and Mavis slipped away in a gig made ready for them by Joseph. Their destination not known.

Two weeks later the newlyweds returned as married farmers. What they had planned a year ago had come to fruition.

They now needed to find a new challenge. Alan would continue to do local shearing and look to improve their flock with new sheep. During his shearing days up north, he had learnt about the necessity to have quality sheep. He had listened to the owners.

With the farm they had purchased one hundred and fifty ewes, one hundred and fifty wethers, and a ram. Alan decided to sell the entire flock and replace it with a good merino flock. Alan, Joseph and Rover drove them to the sale yards, a full day trip.

Alan and James agreed to limit the size of the merino flock to the value of the money earned from the sale of their current flock. The sale day was sunny and had attracted large groups of buyers and sellers. There were thousands of sheep and around fifty to seventy buyers. The auctioneer was quick. They needed to listen or they would miss out on a purchase or worse make a mistake and buy the wrong lot.

Fortunately, their flock sold as a lot and allowed them to purchase a quality ram and one hundred mature merino breeding ewes.

Mavis admired the flock as they drove them down the lane to the main paddock. She could see that the merino flock had larger bodies, were more heavily fleeced than their previous flock and that their anus area had been crutched to protect them from the dreaded flystrike. After the ram was placed in his own paddock, he stopped and assumed a majestic stance as he looked around his new home. Alan hoped he would perform as well he posed.

Time moved quickly and the ewes soon came into season. Alan had painted the belly of the ram with a thick green dye and let him loose in the main paddock with the ewes and left him there to perform.

Alan and Joseph rode around the main paddock and checked the ewes. Nearly all had green dye mark on the rump. The ram had been busy. Five months later the lambs started to drop. Most ewes dropped one lamb, some had twins. A total of eighty-five survived. As soon as the ewes and their lambs had settled down, the flock was driven into the shearing holding paddock and driven through the gateway singularly. All the lambs had their tails docked and, except for four males, the remaining males were marked to become wethers. The four unmarked males would be sold as young rams when they matured. The ewes were inspected and drenched. Alan was pleased with the flock. It was quality, first class.

Shearing time soon arrived, and he recruited James to help, even though they only had a hundred sheep to shear. The lambs would not have a reasonable wool length yet. The merino fleeces were big and bulky with fine wool and required extra care and attention. Alan allowed three days from the time they moved the sheep to the holding pens to complete the full task – shearing, sorting, trimming, rolling, packing, pressing, and branding them with their A over M design in a red dye.

The three workers worked hard and finished the task within the three days, finally returning the sheep to the main paddock. They ended up with five bales of super fine wool.

They loaded the dray with the five bales and delivered the consignment to the railway station for delivery to Elders Wool Brokers for auction at the Melbourne wool sales.

James had enjoyed being involved in the shearing and was beginning to feel like a gentleman farmer, the friendly name Alan had given him, particularly after they received a cheque for forty-four pounds from the wool clip. The lamb drop had increased their flock to nearly two hundred fine merinos. Their farmland had access to water and was well grassed most of the year and could handle a flock of this size without any restriction. The three of them were happy with their decision to buy this farm.

The river had a small open area on the bank on their side of the river. Joseph had built a picnic table, complete with bench seats from left over planks from the extension project and made the area a picnic place.

On a warm sunny day, Mavis often packed a hamper for the couple to stroll arm in arm down to the picnic place to enjoy the peace and tranquillity of the rushing water and listen to the noisy birds perched in the beautiful flowering gum trees growing at the water's edge. The sunlight filtering through the branches completed the picturesque scene.

Fish were plentiful and sometimes trout could be seen jumping into the air. The couple would try their luck and attempt to catch one for a meal. Their rods were made from the branches of spindly fruit trees, pruned to encourage the tree to become thicker. The line was twine used to sew bags and the hooks were purchased at the town's general store. Bait was a problem at times. They found the best way was to lay a hessian bag on the ground in the orchard and keep it damp for a week or two. Normally when the bag was lifted and the clods of soil dug out, worms would be hanging out of the moist clumps of the soil. They only ever caught a few fish.

One day Joseph came down, accompanied by the dog. He sat and watched them quietly. Eventually he came over and asked, 'Have you heard of "trout tickling"?' Alan shook his head and waited for Joseph to explain. 'It has been practised for years in the north of England. The fisherman stands in waist high slow moving water. You put your hand between your spread legs and twiddle your fingers slowly. If you're lucky, an inquisitive trout will get close and a quick finger or two into the gills will allow you to flick the fish onto the bank. It's not easy but I have seen it done.'

Alan asked, 'Are you suggesting we try to "tickle the trout" in the back water over there in the bend?'

Joseph nodded and they walked to the bend where the river meandered. The water at the inner bend was almost still, while the water flow on the outer side of the bend was rapid. Joseph went to the water's edge and stood there quietly looking into the water. He nodded and walked slowly into the water nearly up to his waist and stood still.

Alan sat on the bank with the dog by his side. After about ten minutes Joseph turned his head towards Alan and shook it, ready to give up, when the next second he flicked a fish into the air, but it didn't reach the bank and rapidly swam away.

Joseph left the river, 'Well, that was close, but I'm freezing. I've had enough for today. Your turn next time.' They headed back up the hill to the farmhouse.

James had collected the mail from the coach station and was sitting at the kitchen table looking a little perplexed. When Alan walked in, he immediately asked him if he had heard that the council was planning to erect a dam on the other side of the captain's property. They both knew that land was crown land. What had caused this issue? Generally, the council was non-controversial.

Damming a river would be a major issue. It would affect many downstream farmers who needed the water as a resource. James decided to do some snooping and see if a party or individuals would benefit from the dam proposal.

The council said that they were damming the river with a bank of ten feet across the river with a sluice for the overflow to better serve the farms downstream. But primarily it was to be a reservoir for future district droughts and provide a better flow rate and pressure to the town water supply.

James went to work. Firstly, he decided to obtain a survey map. He needed to know the heights of the local terrain. Secondly, he needed to know the names of the farmers upstream. Could they be involved with the council? He obtained the map from the Melbourne Lands Department. Obtaining the names of the property owners was more difficult to get and would take more time. Some farms were owned by companies with some registered in Sydney.

He, Alan and Joseph, with his experience in military engineering and his map reading knowledge, spread out the map on the kitchen table and examined it in detail. The topographical maps showed four upstream farms would have more water over their properties. Coincidently, the top two of these farms had poor dams and were owned by companies. Joseph worked out that a dam wall of six feet would only increase the water level to the two lower properties but would still adequately increase the water flow rate and pressure of the town water supply.

Why had the council later decided on the ten foot dam? James focused on the top two farms. He managed to obtain the names of the shareholders of one property in Melbourne, but he would have to wait for a reply from Sydney for the other company. He would approach the manager. He didn't want anyone knowing they were being investigated. He was worried if they found out, they would push the council to accelerate the building of the dam. The list of shareholders of the first property were wealthy Melbourne businessmen and appeared to be above suspicion. The property was profitable. They were breeding racehorses. The second property was a sheep run. James now had sufficient experience to recognise that it was only an average class flock. Was it successful?

Alan and James attended a sponsored council meeting called by them to explain the reasons for the reservoir and to answer any submitted questions. The councillors sat in a row of seats up on the Mechanics Institute Hall stage. All looked very superior. James stood up, said which farm he was from and began to ask for an explanation which had arisen from a submitted question. The deputy mayor ruled him, 'Out of Order', as he had not submitted the question. James queried his ruling and did not force the issue, but he began to watch the performance of the deputy mayor, Raymond Guthrie. He had been in court long enough to sense he had a different agenda from the other councillors. He was strong willed and had been most vocal in his objection to the audience submitted questions.

James began to quietly gather a profile on Councillor Guthrie. He had been born in the district and had been a councillor for ten years. He lived in town in a two-story bluestone house, was married and had four children. He and a partner owned a farm produce store. Their business was viable and provided them with a reasonable living.

Coincidently, James was assigned to hear a case in Ellensvale. It involved a minor case of assault. Richard duly arrived with the paperwork. It appeared to be a typical Saturday night incident due to overindulgence of alcohol.

When they arrived at the court, Councillor Guthrie walked towards them. He nodded, then stopped. He looked at James and asked, 'It was you at the meeting last week?' James nodded. The councillor continued, 'Are you involved here today? I'm a witness.'

James said, 'I'll be seeing you inside then.'

Richard said, 'Sir, time to go.' James nodded and walked into the Mechanics Institute.

Richard called the court to order. James assumed his seat. The charge was read out. The alleged offender pleaded guilty.

The prosecutor read out the police report and advised, 'I have nothing more to add.'

The defence lawyer stood. 'I have a character witness who wishes to speak on behalf of the offender, your honour.'

James nodded agreement.

Richard called, 'Councillor Raymond Guthr ie.'

Guthrie walked to the box and accepted the bible from Richard and read the oath. He handed the bible back to Richard and then looked at the magistrate. When he saw it was James, he went white and nearly collapsed. After a second or two he regained his composure.

After he presented his sworn character reference, Guthrie went to the hotel and had a strong drink.

The case was straight forward. The offender was fined two pounds with no conviction.

James had seen Guthrie's reaction to him being the magistrate. He now felt sure something untoward was afoot. He was determined to look further into Councillor Guthrie's background. He had discovered that two of the councillor's children were attending a private boarding school in Melbourne.

Meanwhile the captain was becoming more upset day by day. James was able to make him calm down, but only for a while. When he saw the builders starting to haul up logs onto the crown land he started drinking heavily. The dam issue had been going on for nearly a month and the start date was fast approaching. He had dynamite and, if he became angry enough, he might use it on the dam wall. James still had not received an answer from Sydney regarding the other company.

Joseph and Alan were in Ellensvale purchasing supplies and were driving past the rectory when the minister's wife saw them and invited them to morning tea. The day was hot and dry, and the tea break was welcomed.

The subject of the reservoir arose, and Milton farm was mentioned. The wife mentioned casually that she had played out there as a young girl. She had been a school friend of the daughter of the now deceased owner. When their father died, she and her two brothers, formed a company and installed a manager. Her friend had ended up married to Councillor Guthrie. The brothers weren't interested in becoming farmers but wanted to keep the family farm. They were businessmen in Melbourne.

When Alan told James this news he was puzzled. Surely Guthrie would not have voted on the reservoir project – conflict of interest? James decided to gain access to the council minutes of tho se meetings. When he read the relevant minutes, he found Councillor Guthrie had correctly left the chamber when voting was carried out on the reservoir project motion. A later amendment was passed extending the height to ten feet. James needed to find the reason why this had been done. Eventually he traced the origin of the ten foot extension to the engineer who designed the initial six foot high dam.

A class action by the farmers downstream for ten miles was threatened against the council. It had been assigned to James to determine if a formal hearing was necessary.

Negotiation between both parties was preferable. He would be excluded himself as a semi-interested party, if a formal hearing were to occur and a legal decision needed to be determined.

James asked Richard to request a meeting with the full council and the engineer. The initial agenda was primarily to find out why the reservoir was required. The proposal presented by the council president for the six foot dam wall and subsequent reservoir was reasonable. Basically, the water flow to the town was only a trickle when the river was low, but when the flood waters raised the river three or four feet, the flow to the town taps was reasonable.

Therefore, the councillors believed the river water supply outlet to the town should be raised; a figure of six feet was proposed.

James did not intend to query the local issues at this stage. He was more interested in the reason for the height extension to ten feet.

The president of the council answered. 'The engineer proposed this extension. It would be more appropriate for him to give his reasons.'

James looked at Councillor Guthrie who appeared somewhat uncomfortable, constantly shuffling the papers in front of him.

The engineer presented a small model of the dam sitting on a topographical map with the heights marked in different colours. He began by pointing out the various farms and their heights. He then described the method of building the ten foot dam wall. The river would be partially diverted and a hill alongside the river would be dug up and poured into the river bed with logs imbedded in the soil.

James interrupted, 'Did the design of the dam wall need to be changed when you decided to increase the height to ten feet?' The answer was 'No.'

James continued, 'What was the reason the dam height was increased and by whom?'

No one answered. James asked again. 'Someone must have proposed the dam height be raised. There must have been a reason.'

Silence still. James stood up. 'We'll adjourn now and meet here tomorrow at ten a.m. Thank you.' He and Richard left the meeting, leaving an unsettled group who were unsure how to answer the question. They could see what James was aiming at – why the extra cost? There had to be a reason.

The engineer and Guthrie left immediately after James and Richard, meeting for dinner in a hotel room. Guthrie had talked the engineer into raising the dam wall saying the extra water reserve would be welcomed by all and then encouraged the engineer to convince the other councillors. He had not anticipated the extent of the anger from the farmers and the wrong effect it would have on the image of the councillors, particularly in an election year. The engineer was also in a bind – he had accepted a gratuity.

When the engineer and Guthrie had left the meeting, the remaining councillors had an in-depth conference. They decided to amend the dam height to the original six feet. Hopefully this would appease the farmers and they would withdraw their objection. They all agreed their original reason for the reservoir was valid. The president would formalise their decision at the meeting in the morning.

Prior to the agreed ten a.m. meeting, the president had a meeting with the councillors and he advised all that the ten-foot amendment would be withdrawn at the next council meeting.

Councillor Guthrie realised all of his fellow councillors had made their decision. His manipulation had been subtle, but they had guessed. He decided to resign as they all knew his wife was a shareholder in an involved property. They had trusted him to be neutral but with a magistrate investigating the council they wanted him out and he had obliged them.

Coincidently the engineer left town that morning, back to Melbourne and did not return. He was formally sacked anyhow.

When James and Richard attended the chamber, the president requested to address the assembly. He advised that the council had agreed to amend the reservoir height to six feet. The president advised that the engineer had convinced the council of the now debatable cost benefits of a higher pressure head of water with a ten-foot high reservoir.

While a six-foot reservoir would have been adequate they unfortunately had accepted his specialised knowledge. Councillor Guthrie had tendered his resignation and the engineer had left.

Privately, when several councillors saw the final topographical map, they saw the extent of the backwater and felt they had been had but didn't know how to get out of their predicament. James had forced the issue and helped resolve their error of judgement.

James made out his report and after another council meeting with the local people, they supported the six-foot dam wall proposal and withdrew their class action. He recommended no further action should be taken.

The new engineer used the original drawings and installed another supply pipe two foot above the current one. When the reservoir filled, the town had their increased flow with the two pipes and higher pressure of water.

Alan and James guessed that Guthrie was intending to improve the grass and water access for the sheep, with a view to restocking and increasing the property profitability. Unfortunately, he had had to withdraw his children from boarding school in their last year. Ironically, they went to work on the farm and were happy young farmers. Guthrie did not enter public service again. He continued as a local merchant and seemed happy with his lot in life. He was more naïve than unscrupulous.

CHAPTER SIX

Dreams Achieved

James walked into the courthouse and waved to the duty attendant and the constables in the foyer. The lists for the week's hearings were on the noticeboard. One, in particular, caught his eye – the Crown versus the Voyage Mortgage Investment Company. He remembered reading in the local paper some months ago of an alleged fraud associated with this trading company. Ten thousand pounds had vanished from their account, either stock or money, and the company directors were being sued by the shareholders.

When he reached his office, a court clerk was waiting for him. He greeted him and advised that Chief Magistrate Michael Lynch required his presence in his office. James immediately wondered why. He feared that he had erred in a decision in some way. The clerk led him to his office, opened the door for him to enter, closed the door behind and left.

The chief magistrate stood up, welcomed him and introduced him to two rather official looking gentlemen – Sir Edgar Rainbow and Mr Edmund Smythe. The chief magistrate gestured all to be seated. He told James he had assigned him to be involved in the Voyage Mortgage Investment Company fraud case and to do some specific investigation on behalf of the Crown.

He had been selected as he was relatively unknown to the Victorian Court system, and his job application detailed his High Court relevant experience in the English system. The investigation was to be confidential and he was to report only to him. Sir Edgar was a major shareholder and Mr Smythe was a non-executive director. They would ensure he would not be obstructed. James was handed a large folio of papers. A quick glance showed they had the company letterhead.

The chief magistrate finished, saying, 'Read these and report here tomorrow at the same time.' He was a man of few words.

James replied, 'Thank you' and walked back to his office, wondering where he would start.

The reading of the reports was interesting. The bulk of the reports were related to the movement of funds. The company bought and sold anything marketable. Many of the payments and purchases were cash and duly invoiced. The money trail was very difficult to follow. It reminded James of a similar situation with the Bank of England where the culprits had been splitting transactions every third and fourth money movement and causing confusion with their accounting procedures. Eventually the truth came out and the missing money was located in a bogus account. It had not left the bank.

The next morning, he reported to the chief magistrate's office. Sir Edgar and Mr Smythe were already in attendance. James was asked to give his thoughts.

He started by relating the Bank of England story. He could see they were impressed. He told them that he needed to try to identify suspect transactions and any associated names. After an hour or so the clerk was requested to serve tea during a break in the meeting. The trio agreed James should start immediately on his investigation and use his own initiative without their input. He was to report back, same time and place on Monday's. Mr Smythe gave him a letter of introduction stating that he was a court officer authorised to verify stock levels. The clerk cleared the table and they all left the office.

James was happy with the reception given him by the manager, who promised any staff assistance he might require in the warehouse audit. He then read the letter from Mr Smythe and acknowledged the contents. During the week, James only noticed one deficiency. An order for timber that had two consignment notes raised but James was only able to locate one invoice.

It reminded him of the England crime. He wrote a short but accurate report for the trio and presented it on Monday. However, he mentioned that the manager knew of his requirement to visit the warehouse before he handed over his letter of introduction explaining his mission.

The trio each denied mentioning this outside this office. James said to the chief magistrate that the only other person who knew his mission was the clerk who served the tea. They sat there, shocked – an employee of the Justice Department! They did not have tea that morning. The trio agreed that James continue with the warehouse ploy and report again in one week. The court case was due in three weeks.

James identified two more cases of separated consignments. It took a lot of sorting through the invoices but finally, he identified two names. He removed all the paperwork relating to the transactions and locked them in his office for his further action when he returned after the weekend. When he reported this to the trio, it was agreed that a trap would be set. Tea was requested and, while the clerk was present, James mentioned that he had found some possible incriminating paperwork in the outwards invoices file covering the last six months.

On Monday, as he approached the warehouse, the manager was walking fast towards him. He told him that he had been called to the warehouse Sunday afternoon and found that a small fire had destroyed some paperwork in the office, and he hoped it wouldn't disrupt his stock check. James told him that he needn't worry as he already had the paperwork that he needed and today would be his last day there. He only needed to see if the orders matched the invoices and the bank statements. The manager walked away without saying a word.

The following Monday, when James walked up the courthouse steps, the attendant greeted him and advised him that he had a visitor waiting outside his office. The visitor was the manager who was dishevelled and unshaven. He had come to admit his role in the fraud. James took him to the chief magistrate's office for his normal Monday meeting. He introduced the manager and then asked him to tell the trio his story.

The manager told of how a small theft, that was easy, had then progressed to major fraud. He would split specific consignments with an accounts department friend who handled invoices. The clerk would then duplicate and falsify them. He also admitted that some of the money was in cash at his home. When he was asked about the clerk who served tea, he said, 'He's my brother-in-law.'

The trio sat there just looking at each other, shaking their heads. The trial would be straight forward now that they had a culprit admitting guilt. The police arrived and arrested the manager, then formally charged him. Later that day, the friend was also arrested and charged.

The trio and James sat down and had tea, albeit with a different clerk serving. The chief magistrate thanked James and advised him he would recommend the prosecutor to invite him to join the fraud trial team, as he knew more about the case than anyone else. Possibly he may even be given lead in some parts of the trial.

James sat outside his cottage with an ale. The last few weeks had gone like a blur. It was hard to believe his good fortune. The case had been in the public domain and James had his portrait drawn by a newspaper artist and, together with a small article written on his career, he made the front page. It was a good likeness. Richard pinned the front page on the notice board.

Richard had recovered from his gunshot wound and had returned to work. James had used casual clerks in his absence and kept his position open for him. He collected the mail, notices and went by the chief clerk's office to collect any briefs or case notes for James to action or consider. The other papers were for James, a few reports to finish and a letter from the prosecutor's office.

James was excited to receive a letter from this esteemed office and was delighted when it requested him to make an appointment with the prosecutor's secretary within two days.

When Sean reached the shelter of the dense brush he headed into the deep forest. He had tried his hand at poaching as a young man in Ireland and was confident that he could do the same in the Victorian countryside. The first night he slept in the hollow of a tree.

At sun-up, he found he was within a mile or so of a small farmhouse. He sat and watched, waiting for a sign of life. Mid-morning a farmer left the farmhouse, saddled a horse and rode out over a distant hill, followed by two yelping dogs.

Around noon Sean walked to the back door, armed with a short, thick branch and knocked. There was no answer. He opened the door and slowly entered the farmhouse. The kitchen table had one cup and bowl; the farmer was living alone. Sean quickly searched the three rooms. First, he changed from his prison clothes to some farm clothes. He then found a bag and packed it with more clothes including a high-quality suit and shirt, plenty of food and a loaded revolver. A drawer contained two one-pound notes and some coins; these he pocketed. Whistling an Irish tune to himself, he contently walked back to the forest. He moved further away from the area where he had escaped, turning south towards Melbourne.

The farmer reported the robbery to the police and handed them a completed list of the items stolen. The only item he really valued was the quality suit which his late wife had purchased for him in Rio De Janiero during their voyage to Victoria.

Sean eventually came upon a deserted dilapidated one room hut on a small creek, high up in the hills. He lived in it for two weeks, surviving on his stolen food stocks and trapping possums for meat, knowing full well the police would be after him. He couldn't stay there forever. That day soon arrived.

The deep barking of dogs in the valley disturbed his solitude; his peace and isolation were gone. Lower down, he could see the blue coated horsemen combing the hillside – constables and dogs. He quickly collected his gear and headed over the other side of the hill. He decided to head to Melbourne and started to walk. He knew that, together, the black trackers and the hounds would soon locate him if he stayed in the bush. It would only be a matter of time before he was caught.

Within two weeks he had reached Melbourne and was now able to mingle unnoticed in the crowd. He had shaved his beard and now kept his face clean shaven. He had first grown the beard when he left Ireland. Apart from the occasional trim his beard had been left untouched until now. He was unrecognisable, or almost. His limp was still noticeable.

He had a job as a cleaner and rented a room and a stable in Richmond. On his walk down to Melbourne he had found an unbranded, saddled horse outside an inn at Essendon and had stolen it and put his own brand on it. This was the horse he was riding when he was recognised by Alan.

Sean had started to go out in the evening, locating where the various upper-class clubs were situated. He identified the uptown clubs most of the wealthy patrons frequented. He believed these club members would be easy marks for a mugging.

He soon put his plan into action. Dressed in his stolen suit and shirt he began to mingle and chat with members outside a selected busy club, late in the evening. Eventually he would spot his mark. He would follow the departing inebriated club member and, if he entered a dark laneway, he would cosh him and then rob him of his money.

Sean was just another well-dressed man about town. He kept his muggings to around one a week. Most persons who were robbed were too embarrassed to report the mugging to the police. Sean continued his muggings for three months without notice until he robbed one person twice.

This time he reported the muggings to the police and to his club. This news brought other club members forward, who had been mugged, and a police investigation was initiated.

Sean's cleaning job took him to visit many Victorian buildings, including the courthouse. It wasn't until he saw a drawing of James in the newspaper that his hatred for people in authority resurfaced. He had no control over his mental faculties. He became a man obsessed. He now remembered James as the victim of the botched and hopeless kidnapping attempt by himself and the Marsh brothers. He wondered how the brothers were fairing. He guessed they would be hanged, but, they had, in fact, been sentenced to life imprisonment with hard labour in Pentridge Prison in Melbourne.

Sean reasoned that if he continued cleaning the government buildings, on the days he visited the courthouse he would one day see James and he would then follow him and shoot him. He always carried the stolen loaded revolver.

He changed his mind when he saw James's name on the daily court hearing list. Sean did not go to work. He dressed in the good suit and shirt he had stolen and visited the court as an observer. He sat in the back row and just stared at James as he presided over the court.

Sean was having trouble keeping control of his temper, particularly as James seemed so calm handling the court proceedings. At the noon adjournment, he returned to his Richmond room and slowly calmed down. He decided to make his move at James's next sitting.

Alan needed to meet with the broker to finalise an agreed wool price. James left it to him to negotiate. The talks did not take long, and the secretary prepared the contract to be signed by each of the three parties. Alan strolled over to the courthouse with the paperwork for James's signature. He was late and would have to wait for the noon adjournment to gain access to James. He collected his mail. One was from Inspector Dodson and he was pleased to find out the inspector was still looking for Sean. He thought a recent robbery at a farm in the escape district could have been by him. He had several constables, a black tracker and two hounds searching for the elusive escapee.

The courtroom had several observers, some were relatives and others just curious members of the public. A few women but mainly men. A well-dressed man sitting in the corner attracted Alan's interest. The man had his coat high around his lower face. Alan kept watching him, he wasn't sure why.

Richard entered the court and asked all to rise. James walked in through a rear door and bowed to the courtroom and sat behind an imposing bench. The man in the corner suddenly stood up and briefly turned towards Alan. It was Sean Kennedy! The man moved towards the bench and withdrew a revolver.

Alan shouted, 'He has a revolver.' A nearby constable dived at Sean as he fired. The bullet hit the constable in the shoulder. Sean fired again the second bullet hit a desk. James had ducked behind the bench. The court observers were crowding the main door attempting to escape from the courtroom.

Sean was now acting like a trapped rabbit. He frantically looked left and right and then headed for a side door, as more police pushed their way through the frightened exiting observers.

Sean found himself in the corridor of the administration section which was lined with offices. He ran to the end of the corridor and vanished. More police arrived and blocked the street exits. Sean was trapped, but where was he? Inspector Dodson arrived and took charge. A map of the courthouse building was laid out on a large table and the inspector detailed teams to systematically search each room, one after another. The progress was slow; caution was required as they knew Sean was armed.

The constables each had a shotgun which gave them a decided advantage if there was to be a gun fight. The search was becoming frustrating. Nearly every room was checked without success.

Finally, they located one room where the manhole cover had moved. The desk below it had dust clumps on it and was the only dusty desk in the room. Inspector Dodson asked for a dog to be brought to the room. It was lifted into the ceiling area. It soon came back wagging its tail. Sean was not in the ceiling. Where had he gone?

The inspector looked at the building map again. 'How many rooms have we not searched? See these ones here. What are they?'

'These three are holding cells and that one is the records room. It has no windows and it's locked from the corridor,' one of the court officials answered.

The inspector said, 'I think I know where he is. Look at the map. There are only two manholes. Look where the other one is. It's over the records room. I do not want any shooting unless absolutely necessary. Is that clear? I want to smoke him out. I want a smoke bomb. A large bundle of cotton waste soaked with whale oil should generate plenty of smoke. And put a weight on the manhole cover. We don't want him to escape again.'

Within fifteen minutes all was ready. Two lengths of ropes about twenty feet long were attached to the bundle. One rope had a large rock tied to one end. A short rope was tied to the door handle. The cotton waste was set alight.

A strong constable swung a large hammer and smashed the door lock. He then pushed the door open, which immediately prompted two revolver shots. The shots confirmed the inspector's assumption as to Sean's whereabouts. Another constable slung the rock deep into the records room and pulled the door closed with the short rope.

After a few minutes, a choking Sean called, 'I'm coming out, don't shoot.'

'Throw out your revolver first.' The revolver came skidding out on the floor, quickly followed by a staggering, gasping Sean.

A constable dragged the cotton waste out of the records room by the other long rope and threw it out of a corridor window to some constables outside the building, who smothered the smoke bomb. The inspector had thought of everything.

The inspector called a meeting of those involved in the court shooting and the capture incident. James and Alan were included. The inspector gave a summary of what he knew of the prisoner and asked Alan to fill in some details of his Irish background and the killing of the Waterford mayor. He then asked James to relate his kidnapping experience. A court scribe was kept busy recording all the information. After two hours of crosstalk a definitive profile of Sean Kennedy had been compiled. Well, not really. Sean surprisingly cared for his horse and asked the police to go feed and water him.

At the stables a young man asked where the horse owner was. When told he was in police custody, he said he was the landlord and asked, 'Who's going to pay for his room?' The police then went to his room to pack and remove everything, excluding furniture, and took it back to the police barracks to catalogue it. A copy of the list of Sean's effects was attached to his now extensive file.

When Sean's effects were being checked into the evidence room, a sharp eyed constable spotted the suit and wondered how a cleaner could afford such expensive clothing. When he examined the coat, he found a label – Made in Brazil.

He mentioned it to Inspector Dodson who asked Sean, 'Where did you get it?'

He said he had bought it in Ireland from a local tailor. Sean was unaware of the label in the pocket.

The constable said, 'The victims of the muggings reported a similar colour and patterned suit, but he had a moustache. Could he be the mugger?'

Inspector Dodson said, 'Have another look around his room. Don't forget the mugger had a moustache. You might be wrong.' The constable searched the room and the attic without any luck.

The constable walked to the stable and, while giving the horse a pat as it was feeding, he noticed a section of canvas poking out from under the chaff. He pushed the horse back and tugged on the canvas. It was a bag. In it he found a false moustache and a wig. His suspicion had been correct.

The inspector was delighted and laughed. 'Let's see what he has to say now.'

Sean didn't respond; he just sat there smiling.

The inspector knew he did not have sufficient evidence to charge him. He decided to have a line up. Five constables with a moustache and dressed in dark suits similar to the stolen one and with Sean dressed in the actual stolen suit wearing the false moustache. The victims of the muggings all said they had seen Sean around the clubs but couldn't say for certain if he was the culprit. With the 'attempt to kill' court case imminent, the inspector decided to concentrate on this charge only and he placed the possible associated charges and the mugging cases on his back burner.

James and Richard were naturally called as witnesses. When Sean entered the court, he was chained and seemed totally oblivious to the seriousness of the charge. He was looking around, waving and smiling to all and sundry. James wondered about his mental stability. The judge was gruff and experienced. As soon as he saw Sean, he decided that he was acting as an unstable person and would not to be swayed by his antics.

The prosecutor had prepared a strong case based on the evidence provided by Inspector Dodson and his team. His trial would be conducted and decided by the judge only. It progressed smoothly without any real defence being entered by his lawyer.

Sean was hoping his mental act would be a strong consideration for clemency. He feigned loss of memory, laughed without reason and talked loudly in Gaelic. But when his previous alleged crimes were entered into evidence in detail, he realised he was doomed.

The judge summarised the proceedings. He looked solemn. 'Sean Kennedy, please stand.' He paused and continued. 'I find you guilty of attempting to kill James Newton. Do you have anything to say before I pass sentence on you?'

Sean was standing very still and thought for a moment before answering. 'I will be remembered for my deeds when the rest of you will have long been forgotten.'

The judge said, 'I hereby sentence you to be hanged by your neck until you are dead. May God have mercy on your soul.' The judge stood, bowed and left the courtroom.

Sean was taken by the arm. He was motionless for a few seconds and then went with the constable down to the holding cells. He was to be hanged in three weeks.

Sean was transported to Pentridge Jail and taken to the condemned offender's cell. He seemed to accept his fate and behaved friendly to his jailors.

Two days before his scheduled execution, he began vomiting. This illness lasted continuously throughout the day. Early evening, he collapsed unconscious. The duty warden decided to call for a wagon and take him in shackles to the Melbourne Hospital. Even though he was to be hanged, he didn't want him to die on his watch.

The warden who sat in the wagon with Sean kept checking to see if he was still alive, although unconscious.

The duty hospital doctor was old school. He agreed Sean could be put in a private room on the first floor, but he totally objected to a patient being shackled in his hospital. He pointed out that there was only one entry and the two wardens could be positioned outside the door.

A nurse began to prepare Sean for the doctor's inspection. He used a pin to prick Sean's arm several times to check his reaction and confirm his unconscious state. Sean did not move. The doctor then asked the nurse to bring a fluid drip from the ground floor.

Immediately she left, when the doctor had his back turned, Sean left his bed and struck the doctor a savage blow to the back of his neck, knocking him unconscious. Sean went to the window pushed it open and climbed out onto the roof. He crept along the gutter until he came to be above a large hedge. He jumped into it and escaped into the dark night.

He headed to an old disused stable he knew of and, on the way, he collected a change of clothes from someone's clothesline. Later he went back to his stable and collected another revolver from under the stable straw. The prison authorities later discovered Sean had been hoarding salt and after mixing it in water, had drunk it and this had caused the violent vomiting. He had cleverly feigned unconsciousness.

James and Richard both had felt uncomfortable hearing the death sentence pronounced. They had a few quiet drinks each with their own thoughts. Alan went back to the farm to prepare for the Annual Agriculture Show and James back to his office. Life soon returned to normal.

James had his appointment with the prosecutor's office and was delighted to be invited onto the team for the fraud case against the Voyage Mortgage Investment Company. This was a chance to further his experience in the corporate field and up his image in the Victorian judicial system. His London experience had been of a high standard but was limited. He hoped his input would be of value to the team and he would also learn from the experience.

The lead up to the fraud hearing consisted of a meeting with the prosecutor's staff, clerks and researchers. James sat quietly and listened. There seemed to be a lot of duplication of discussion.

The chairman asked, 'James, would you care to comment on what you think of our approach.'

James mentioned the duplication issue.

Surprising the chairman laughingly agreed. 'Yes, the meeting has gone on for too long, with little progress. Let's break for ten minutes and come back more focused.' The remainder of the pre-hearing preparation meeting was completed that day.

James's anticipation for the case was rudely interrupted when he was visited by the chief clerk, who advised him, 'The manager of Voyager Mortgage Investment Company committed suicide last night and his brother-in-law has vanished.' The prosecutor's clerk came down later and thanked him for his involvement. He had now been reassigned back to the magistrates court. He would be invited again in the future as required for similar cases.

He was naturally disappointed but the same morning he received the news that Sean Kennedy had escaped. This news stunned him. How could a convicted criminal escape from the main Melbourne jail confines? It shocked James after what he had been through.

Inspector Dodson offered him a bodyguard. Had Sean remained in Melbourne or jumped a ship? He could be miles away. James now also carried a revolver in a shoulder holster. He had a bodyguard only when in the courthouse. James gradually began to relax and stopped looking over his shoulder all day.

James was talking with Alan, outside the courthouse. The captain had come over a day early for his normal weekly chat with Alan, accompanied by his favourite bottle of whisky. He said he had a few nips already. He had received a letter advising him of his acceptance into the Stella Maris House for Retired Merchant Seamen in Melbourne and wanted to celebrate the good news with his neighbour.

After pouring two drinks he asked Alan, 'I'm going to sell my farm. Do you want to buy it? You and James can have first offer at a reduced cost seeing we're friends and neighbours.'

'Yes, we could be interested. I will talk it over with James and get back to you,' replied Alan.

James was very interested and began thinking of what they should offer as a reasonable price. Their company was financial, with a cash holding of two hundred and ten pounds.

Would that be sufficient? The partners had spoken

of expanding their property holdings next year. Were they ready to expand now?

A four-wheel coach was cantering down the street when two dogs started fighting and ran out in front of the coach and spooked the horse. It reared and darted towards the footpath where Alan and James were standing. The coach nearside wheel hit James and knocked him to the ground. Slightly stunned, he sat there with Alan tending him.

The coach driver alighted quickly and bent over James. 'Are you injured? I am so sorry. It happened so quickly. I couldn't stop him in time.'

James looked up to see a well-attired very attractive young lady.

Alan helped James to his feet and then tied the horse to a nearby post and placed its feed bag on its head.

James answered, 'I'm a bit shaken but that's all. I'm fine.'

When Alan was satisfied James was in good hands, he said, 'Goodbye, I'll see you at the farm at the weekend.'

The young lady introduced herself as Fiona Giles and he replied, 'James Newman'. They mutually decided to adjourn to the courthouse tearooms. After placing their order, they sat at a corner table.

James looked at Fiona. 'At a guess I believe you could be from a farm. I noticed the farm soil on the coach wheels. You are Australian born by your speech and, by your complexion, you spend time outdoors. How close am I?'

Fiona laughed. 'Very good. My turn. You are a part time farmer; your friend gave you away. You work in this courthouse – the doorman acknowledged you – and you're English educated, probably from the north. My father came from Cumberland, so I recognise the accent.'

James nodded and clapped her astute assessment.

Fiona asked, 'Where is your farm?'

He replied, 'The friend you saw me with is a partner in a farm we share outside Ellensvale, a small town north of Melbourne. Ironically, today when we met, we were discussing expanding our holdings.'

Fiona shook her head. 'You won't believe this, but I share a farm with my two brothers about ten plus miles west of Ellensvale. We moved there two years ago from Melbourne. My family had a department store but when my father entered the public service, we sold up and my brothers and I became beef cattle and pig breeders. My father and my mother still live in Melbourne. I am on my way to have lunch with them today. Actually, I'm running late now. I am sorry but I will have to go.'

James sat there listening to this delightful, confident and attractive young lady. He wanted to meet her again. He stood up and walked her to her coach. 'I would like to meet with you again. May I?' He waited.

She replied, 'I would like that. We're having a birthday get-together at the farm next Saturday at noon for my elder brother, William. Please come along. The farm's name is *Cumberland* and it's well signed on the Western Road. Goodbye for now.'

He waved and she waved back to him.

When James arrived home Friday evening the three sat down and discussed the viability of purchasing the captain's farm. The farm agreement was to be a walk out–walk in deal. The property comprised one hundred and sixty acres of good soil with a river frontage and it was running sixty head of Hereford beef cattle and twenty pigs, plus two horses. The captain bred the cattle and pigs for meat, and it had a small slaughter house and packing room.

The local butcher and the captain had a financial

arrangement for the butchering and selling of the captain's meat through his butcher shop in town. The captain cleaned and tanned the livestock skins and sold them by auction in Melbourne. It provided the captain with a reasonable income with some left over.

Mavis went to the captain's farmhouse and asked him to show her through the rooms.

The outer walls were part bluestone and weatherboard planks, the interior walls were whitewashed and made of lathe and plaster. The floors were Baltic pine. It was very neat with everything in its place, or as the captain described, 'ship shape'. The furniture was basic but good quality. There were four rooms – a large bedroom, a kitchen-dining room, a laundry-storeroom and a reading room. The kitchen had the stove backing onto the fireplace in the reading room. It was a very cosy home.

There were no ornaments or mementos; perhaps they had been packed already. It did lack a woman's touch. There were few curtains or wall hangings and no flowers. Mavis was impressed with the house; she liked it. At the evening meal Mavis shared her thoughts and comments. The men were pleased with her positive opinion.

Alan and James then went to visit the captain and look around the farm and its chattels. It had two sheds plus the slaughterhouse and a large barn. The barn had two horse stalls, a small forge (used by the previous owner) and an open attic for livestock food storage. A gig and a four-wheel cart were at the other end. The adjacent wall had the bridles, reins and harnesses hanging on it. A few horse rugs were rolled up and stowed in a corner. The barn was dry and airy. The two sheds had bits of old machinery, containers and general odds and ends collected over the years, some left by the previous owner. They thanked the captain and after the inevitable 'wee drop', they walked home.

Well, buy or not? They each agreed the property was in good order and the livestock appeared healthy. They needed to get an expert opinion on the matter. They decided to wait a week and, if they were still happy and could agree on a price, they would make an offer to purchase the property. They asked Joseph if he would move there and manage it, on a wage. He agreed immediately. James said he would move into the cottage and upgrade the furniture and fittings. His current room could be used as a guest room.

James decided to take up Fiona's offer to visit her on her brother's birthday. He had purchased a few charcoal prints of Hobson's Bay. He would take one as a birthday present to her brother. He estimated that the ride would take a few hours. He would have to ride back towards town to join the Western Road and then keep the river on his right. To the best of his knowledge there were no bridges to cut short his trip. The river meandered away from the road for a few miles then rejoined it, continuing west.

James departed Woodlea early morning, riding Tess. He was excited and was looking forward to seeing Fiona again. He hadn't met a person like her before. In the short time he had spent with her he had found her to be so natural, relaxed and, importantly, very attractive.

The day was fresh, and he wore a sheepskin coat and bush hat to keep warm. After an hour's riding he dismounted and walked for ten minutes to exercise his leg muscles. James joined the Western Road just north of Ellensvale and turned right. The road was wider and better maintained than most roads. It was a popular road used by vehicles, horses and the ever-optimistic miners, even though the major gold rush days were over.

Two hours into his ride he saw a sign – *Cumberland Estate 4 miles*. The road continued straight on while the river slowly bent in a north-west direction. A mile or two further on, he could see a large herd of fat black cattle and further on, a large farmhouse, two smaller matching houses, an enormous barn and several other sheds. The river flowed in the background. He eventually came to a gateway with the sign – *Cumberland Estate* – and he headed to the buildings. As he got closer, he could see people milling around a large tent. He continued to the row of tethered horses, looking at the group and searching for Fiona. He heard a voice call his name and was relieved to see her. He dismounted as she welcomed him with a peck on the cheek.

He said, 'I was little nervous riding into your property.'

'I was hoping you would come,' she said. 'Tie up your horse and let's meet my brothers.'

They walked to a group of men talking and drinking. Fiona introduced her brothers, Winston and William.

James recognised William as a local councillor from the prior council meetings.

The councillor also recognised him. 'Welcome to Cumberland.' He paused. 'Am I correct, you're the magistrate who sorted out the reservoir issue?'

James answered, 'Yes, it was me. I hope that is not a problem.'

'Goodness me, no. You did the council and the community a favour. Now would you like a beer?' William replied. James nodded.

Fiona was looking at him in a strange way. 'Why didn't you tell me you were a magistrate? I thought you were a court clerk.'

James laughed. 'Why didn't you guess? You were accurate on the other guesses.'

Fiona smiled. 'I'm not perfect. Let me show you around.' They walked to the large house and entered. It was red brick outside. Inside, the walls were covered in plaster and wallpaper with wood panelled sections and complimented by polished wooden floors. The walls were decorated with paintings and etchings. The furniture was nearly all walnut – chaise lounges and chairs covered with rich coloured velour material and velvet and damask curtains. A grand piano was in the corner of the main room. Everything breathed quality.

'My older married brother, Winston, lives here. William and I have the other houses as our homes. The three houses were all built similarly inside and out. As I said, my parents live in Melbourne. They couldn't be here today,' Fiona said. 'My father and mother are attending an intercolonial conference in Sydney. My father is presenting a financial paper. Mother always travels with him.'

James asked, ' When did your parents come to the colonies?'

'They sold their family estate over twenty-five years ago and immigrated here. They settled in Sydney at first, where I was born. I did most of my education overseas in England and then studied art in Paris. The family then came to Melbourne a few years before the gold rush and established a department store. They made a lot of money supplying the would-be miners. They sold the department store and built a home in St Kilda and this farm. Father called it *Cumberland Estate* after his home in Carlisle, North England. We have six hundred acres and run up to three hundred head of cattle after the calves come in. We sell once a year and change our bull every two years. It will be a few years before we know our profitability. But we have other assets, so we are not too concerned.'

Fiona stopped. 'I've spoken enough; over to you.'

While walking they had come to Fiona's home and entered. She led him to a large sunny room. It was her studio. They sat down, looking at the walls. The walls were full of sketches by her. James was no expert, but he could see she was a very accomplished artist.

James looked at her. 'My parents are Yeomen farmers dating back hundreds of years. I didn't dislike farming, but I didn't want to be tied down to a farm for life, so I did law at Manchester University. I wanted a change of lifestyle and a warmer climate. I enjoyed my legal career but when an opportunity came to join the Colonial Legal Service I applied, and here I am. The farm happened by accident. Believe it or not I was kidnapped, and Alan was instrumental in my rescue. He wanted a farm and I helped provide some capital, so we formed a company and became farmers, although I would be classed as a gentleman farmer. He runs the farm and I help as necessary on the business side. We are looking at purchasing the adjacent farm now, but we need the cattle's health checked before we commit. Who checks your cattle?'

Fiona answered, 'We do our own health checks. William has completed a three months course in England at a veterinary school. We'll asked him later.'

James stood up and started looking at her sketches. They were predominately family portraits. He recognised William and Winston. She pointed out her mother. He could see where she obtained her good looks. Her father was dressed in Masonic regalia and looked very officious. He assumed he must be a highly graded member.

Fiona interrupted his thoughts. 'We should join the others. It's time to eat.' She took James's arm.

The brothers and Winston's wife, Anne, were very friendly and made him feel comfortable. The meal was served in the large tent and there was a real picnic atmosphere. James socialised with many other revellers and the beer and the happy party goers soon had James feeling mellow.

Fiona only had one drink. She noticed James's mellowness and suggested that he stay in the guest room in William's house.

James was sufficiently aware of his happy semi-inebriated state and accepted the offer. Moreover, the sun would be setting soon and he would not have reached his home until well after dark. Winston had friends in his guest room as did Fiona.

Fiona took his arm. 'Let's go for a walk to clear your head.'

He nodded in agreement.

They walked in silence to the river bank. She turned suddenly and kissed him. 'I've been wanting to do that all day.'

James did not reply, he just returned the kiss, only for longer. They sat quietly on the river bank looking at the rippling water.

James spoke first. 'I would like to see you again. I must admit you are a very attractive woman but I would have thought you would be in a relationship.'

Fiona replied, 'There was someone. He was drowned at the entrance to Port Phillip Bay in a shipwreck over a year ago. I retreated to the farm and started drawing. It's only since I met you that I have resurfaced, so to speak and, yes, I would like to see you again. I visit mother every two weeks in Melbourne, or you can come here at weekends.'

James nodded. 'I have my mail held at the Ellensvale Coach station. We could keep in contact through there or my courthouse mailbox.'

She smiled. 'Yes, I'd enjoy that. Now let's walk back.'

William settled him in the guestroom and James soon fell asleep. The beer helped.

The morning started with a rooster crowing loudly to all and sundry. A knock on the door announced William. He invited him to join the family in the main house for breakfast in thirty minutes.

As he left William's home, Fiona was walking up the same path going to breakfast. They kissed and walked arm in arm. The breakfast room table was set and had hot dishes on a side table alongside a wall.

Anne escorted James and Fiona to their seats and sat alongside them waiting for William, Winston and the other two guests to join them. Anne proudly advised, nearly all the breakfast food had been grown or bred on the farm – eggs, bacon, milk, vegetables, fruit and orange juice. The others arrived and breakfast was enjoyed.

James took the opportunity to raise the subject of the health inspection of the captain's cattle. William nodded and offered to do the inspection for him. He said he was riding into Ellensvale next week and would be only too happy to help out. He advised only a sample of them needed to be checked. Generally, one in twenty cattle would suffice to satisfy a herd's health and condition inspection.

James had to return to Melbourne the next day and he needed to leave before noon. After thanking Fiona's family for their courtesy, Fiona walked down the drive with him leading Tess. They agreed to meet at the courthouse tearoom Wednesday week. They kissed, he mounted Tess and with a final wave cantered back to the Western Road.

William arrived as expected. Alan had asked the captain if he could have half of his cattle ready for inspection. The captain had looked at William with suspicion. He need not to have worried though. After an hour of inspection his cattle, including a few calves, were given a clean bill of health. The captain asked William to check his new boar.

He said he wasn't sure if he had done his job and didn't think he would be getting any piglets. He was annoyed, as he had paid top price for him. William offered to have a look at the sows.

After half an hour of pushing and feeling the sows, William turned and nodded. 'I think they are all carrying. The boar has done his job; you need not worry. You will have quite a few litters of porkers. Also, I had a good look at your bull. He has a straight pizzle, his testicles are firm and he is well muscled. If you are interested, I'd exchange my bull for yours one day.' The captain just nodded. He was more interested in selling the property as a package, rather than worry about exchanging a bull.

The captain thanked William, brought out the whisky bottle and invited them to join him.

Alan and William rode back to the farm talking about the cattle and pigs. William said the animals were all healthy and good quality. They were a valuable asset to the property. Alan made up his mind to recommend they buy the captain's farm and to start negotiating when James returned at the weekend. William stayed for dinner and remained overnight. He was good company and they talked late into the night.

The Annual Agriculture Show was a highlight of the Ellensvale social calendar. Farmers came from miles away to exhibit their livestock and farm produce, such as vegetables, fruits, home cooking and even their sewing craft skills.

The Shearer and the Magistrate

Alan selected two ewes with lambs and the ram to show. He penned them in the shearing shed for a few weeks prior to the show. He wanted to keep their wool clean and free of grass seeds and dirt. He trimmed their hooves and then polished them. The ram's horns were also polished. They were entered in the Ewe with Lamb, and Fine Wool Ram competitions.

The opening day was a gala day with a parade in the arena of the livestock, carriages, horse riders and officials, accompanied by the local pipe band. Alan had repainted the cart and added some designs to the sides. The leather seat had been recovered, and he had purchased a black harness set ready for the show parade.

During the parade Mavis drove the cart with Tess in her new harness and Rover in the back. Their black cart towed by a black mare in a black harness looked very smart.

Alan walked the haltered ewes and the ram around the arena, waving back to the crowd while the lambs followed their mothers.

The Sheep Hall was huge. It had over two hundred stalls. Their three stalls were in the centre section. They soon arranged a few straw bales to sit on and an area to lie down for a nap while waiting for their turn to parade their sheep.

They took the two ewes to be weighed at the outside scales. When they returned one of the lambs was missing. They had been warned to watch out for lambs being stolen but had not paid any attention. Alan took the ewe, whose lamb was missing, and walked her slowly around the hall. Halfway up the far aisle, his ewe started baaing loudly. This was followed by a lamb baaing. Alan released the ewe. She ran directly to the lamb who was in a pen with other lambs.

A man in the stall, stood up, looking guilty. 'The lamb just wandered in. Sorry.' He opened the pen and let the lamb out. It immediately nuzzled the ewe's teat and started drinking. Alan did not reply. He punched the man in the face, picked up the ewe's halter and walked back to his stall with the lamb following its mother. A few bystanders clapped; it seemed the man was not popular.

Show time arrived. They were nervous as they walked out with the ewes and lambs as two separate entries. They watched how the other exhibitors acted and copied them. As this was their first show, they didn't want to be embarrassed by doing something dumb. The judges walked around the entrants twice, they checked their teeth and the wool quality on the rump and near the belly. The judges were in no hurry and looked their way several times and then referred to their hand boards.

They were not optimistic so were both surprised and delighted when one of the ewe and lamb entries won third place and Mavis was presented with a green ribbon. Alan was so excited he kissed a woman judge. The next event was for Fine Wool Rams. The judges performed the same ritual, walking around inspecting and checking and Alan was again proudly awarded a ribbon. This time a red one for second place. That night they celebrated, dining on sandwiches and champagne in the sheep stall, using a straw bale as a table.

As he was leaving the arena Alan was approached by another farmer who introduced himself as John Smith, President of the Agriculture Society. 'Who worked on your cart? I'd like to meet him. I buy and sell carts and my coach builder has retired. I need another.'

Alan replied, 'I did. I'm a coachbuilder turned farmer. I could be interested. I have a large barn but you would have to come to me. What would you propose?'

John thought for a moment. 'After expenses we split the profit. I've been in local business for ten years and I own the Ellensvale Produce Store.'7

Alan nodded. 'Let me think about it and I'll come and see you next week.' They shook hands and went their separate ways.

Early next morning they loaded the sheep onto the cart and headed home. As they were leaving, Alan was handed a brochure advertising a shearers' meeting there on the final day of the show. He put it in his pocket and headed home.

That evening he sat on the veranda and read the brochure. The shearer's agenda was to form a group to collectively represent their grievances to the station owners.

He decided to attend, more out of interest rather than action. He had heard the shearers' complaints during the evening meal times at the stations and some sounded reasonable. The difference in pay and hours worked between the stations were the major issues. The shearers negotiated them directly with the managers or through contactors.

The room had around fifty shearers when the meeting started. The organisers were shearers and aired their thoughts and took questions, but nothing was really achieved.

A few owners were in attendance as were two contractors. One owner spoke and said if the shearers could form a representative group he would see if he could get a few owners to meet with them and come up with a standard set of rules. They clapped at his response and then began forming a committee.

Alan was pouring a cup of tea when a contractor approached him. He said he was collecting a team of shearers for six months' work from Queensland to Victoria. He said he paid well and was well known.

Alan asked, 'Which sheds?' He reeled off several names of stations. Alan told him he had only heard of one – *Melinda*.

The contractor replied, 'Yes it's a large shed. I've been there. It has forty stands.'

Alan said nothing. He knew it only had thirty stands. Was this contractor mistaken or one of the unscrupulous ones in the industry? He thanked him for the offer but declined to join him.

However, he did write to Fred Green, the manager of *Melinda* and told him of the conversation with this contractor. A few weeks later he received a reply thanking him. His suspicions were correct. The company had been charged for forty shearers and had only been supplied with thirty by this contractor. The company had been signing off invoices on trust. They had not been referring invoices to him for verification. It was poor management. The meeting ensured that Alan would support a shearers group to weed out the industry problems.

Alan told Mavis of the offer for him to do some coachbuilding and, as he had spare time, he had decided to try it for a month or so. He didn't want to be overcommitted as he had *Woodlea* to run and also wanted to continue the local shearing.

He went to the produce store and saw John at the counter.

They went into his office. Alan spoke first. 'I've thought about your coach work offer. I'm happy to give it a go for a month, to see what the workload will be.'

John replied, 'I average around four sales per month and, yes, I can agree with that. I'll supply what you need. I'll have my delivery driver drop past your farm daily as necessary.' They had made a handshake agreement.

Two days later the first cart requiring work arrived. After a month, Alan only had five carts sent to him and they only required a total of four days of work. On the assumption this was a normal workload, Alan agreed to continue on a monthly basis. John was happy with this arrangement and Alan had an additional modest income of thirteen shillings per day.

Joseph walked into the barn. 'The river's still rising. Let's hope there's not too much more snow to be melted in the alps. The lower farms will be in trouble and even that little valley town may be flooded if we get too much more water. The summer rains forecast won't help if they arrive now.'

Alan rode up to the reservoir. Water was now pouring over the top. The side sluice couldn't handle the excess volume it had normally spilled.

As he rode home, he passed the old disused quarry next to the river. It was separated by a sloping strip of land only a hundred yards wide. The quarry opened, on the opposite side of the quarry, to an old dried up creek in a large crown land forest.

When he mentioned this to Joseph, he went to his cottage and returned with the topographical map to confirm what Alan had said.

The next day they both rode to the strip of land. Joseph nodded to himself. He soon came up with a suggestion – use explosives to make a diversion canal to the quarry at the shortest distance. He had experience d similar challenges in his army days.

The strip was three feet above the river water height and had a fall of six feet to the quarry. The explosives would only be required to blast a trench fifty yards long and five yards wide. Joseph advised as the soil was loose, with no rocks, the flood water would scour the trench even wider.

Alan and Joseph rode to the mayor's office and put the plan to him. He immediately agreed and called his works manager to his office. He told him to prepare a demolition team to blast the trench.

The works manager said, 'I'm only approved to do road blasting.'

The mayor replied, 'If you refuse to do this, I will fire you right now. This is an emergency and I'm not waiting for government approval.'

The works manager stared at him in amazement and stuttered, 'Yes, I'll do it. When?'

The mayor answered, 'Now! Meet me at the quarry with your team in three hours.'

Within three hours the explosives team had arrived. They drilled four holes at ten-yard intervals, six feet deep. The charges were laid, and the small crowd moved back to a safe distance.

The works manager pushed the plunger and the dynamite ignited. The noise was deafening. The explosion blasted the ground apart, sending the soil forty feet into the air. A massive dust cloud followed that settled on the watching crowd, making them cough and brush their eyes clear.

As the soil descended, water started to pour from the river and surge into the blasted diversion canal. As Joseph had predicted, the rushing water soon widened the canal.

The mayor immediately sent a rider to the downstream valley town to advise them of the action. Politically he had scored with the electorate with his no-nonsense and positive leadership to the potential flood situation.

The next morning the river had fallen one foot at the river diversion canal and in three days it was down two feet and the water flow over the reservoir had almost ceased. It the summer rains held off the flood risk was over.

Joseph was awarded a Certificate of Appreciation by the Council for his suggestion.

The canal water from the river filled the quarry, then flowed into the old creek bed and spread out into the large forest where the water dispersed and spread out into the low-lying area. Ultimately it would regenerate the forest to its former glory.

As agreed in their last letter, Fiona was taking James to the Australia Club in Collins Street for lunch. He had heard of the club but, as it was for members only, he had not been inside its portals.

Fiona never ceased to amaze him, but he was curious as to her involvement with the club. He waved to her as she drove up in her gig to the courthouse, right on time. He climbed aboard the gig and gave her a peck. She was as pretty as a picture dressed in the latest style. It enhanced her well-shaped figure. The trip up Collins Street was pleasant as they casually chatted away.

The street had recently been surfaced and, with the sun filtering through the trees, it had a delightful continental appearance.

James climbed from the gig, tied the horse to the post at the front of the club and helped Fiona alight. He then went to the gig food box and extracted the horse nosebag and slung it over its head. He dusted his hands and joined Fiona at the entrance.

The doorman tipped his hat. 'Good to see you again, Miss Giles, and welcome, sir.' He held the door open and they entered the large ornate hall leading to the main dining room.

They were approached by the maître de. 'Your table is by the window. Please follow me, madam.'

The table they were seated at overlooked Collins Street. It was a busy street with people, horses and carriages travelling to and fro.

Fiona pointed to a department store on the other side of the street. 'That was our store until a few years ago. It was smaller then. It's since been extended.'

James looked at Fiona. 'Do you mind me asking a question?' She shrugged her shoulders. 'Are you a member here? I was under the impression this was a men's only club.'

Fiona laughed. 'My father pays my brothers and my membership as a present for us each year and it is an *exclusive* club. There is a subtle difference.'

The waiter arrived with a menu mainly written in French. James's French was only schoolboy standard, whereas after living in France for several years, Fiona's was impeccable. She ordered an excellent meal and, as the two of them chattered away, they both realised they were becoming closer.

At the end of the meal Fiona said, 'My parents are having an informal evening at the end of the month. Would you like to accompany me?'

James smiled. 'Of course, I'd be delighted. I'd like to meet them.' They both knew they were approaching an important moment in their lives.

The night had a full moon and the stars were out in full. He wished Fiona was seated alongside him as the hansom cab clip clopped down St Kilda Road. She had said, 'Just tell your driver to take you to *Carlisle*. He will know where it is.'

The driver soon said, 'There's *Carlisle* on the corner, sir.' Alan saw a well-lit, impressive two-story building. Cabs were travelling in and out of the driveway. He alighted and took a deep breath before entering the foyer. A doorman took his hat and cane and walked him to the main entrance where Fiona was talking to another young lady.

She smiled and walked over to him to give him a kiss as soon as she saw him. 'Welcome to *Carlisle*. Come and meet my parents.'

They lined up in a queue. James looked around at the surroundings. It was both a palatial and elegant reception house.

'James, this is my father, Arthur Giles, and my mother, Elizabeth Giles. Father, Mother, this is James Newton.' They shook hands.

'Welcome, James. So, you're the young man Fiona has been telling us about. We will talk more over dinner.'

Fiona led him to a table and introduced him to six other people already seated. They were the youngest at the table. James was to be seated next to her father and her mother on the other side of her.

When Arthur and Elizabeth Giles joined the table the other diners became more vocal. They had been waiting for their hosts to be seated. James suddenly remembered he did not know what the evening was about.

Arthur started, 'Well, James, I've been reading up on you. You made the headlines two weeks ago in the courthouse shooting.'

Obviously, Fiona had not read a newspaper for the last few weeks. She just looked at him with a puzzled expression.

James was somewhat embarrassed when the others all looked at him, waiting for him to comment. 'Yes, it was an unnerving day. I hope not to have another one. Fortunately, the constable is recovering. Fiona, I was going to tell you about it later this evening.'

A doorman approached James and whispered, 'There are gentlemen here who wish to speak with you urgently.'

James looked to the doorway and saw Richard and Inspector Dodson standing there. James stood up and excused himself.

Inspector Dodson handed him a letter. It was from Sean Kennedy.

Attention – Magistrate J Newton.

'I know where you are tonight. I am at the lane on the corner of the Collingwood Town Hall. I have kidnapped a Miss Jane Millingan. (I have included her shawl and necklace). I will exchange her for you. Be at the corner by midnight. I am serious. She is injured, bring a gig. No police. You know who.'

James said nothing for a minute or two. Finally, he looked at Richard. 'Yes, I will go. Richard can you be my driver?'

He nodded. 'But I will borrow your revolver.' James unstrapped his shoulder holster and handed it to Richard.

Inspector Dodson said, 'We will be nearby but out of sight. We don't want you being kidnapped again. We need to get going. We have a few more things to do.'

James went back to Fiona and kissed her. 'It's urgent; I must go. I'll try to get back tonight.'

Fiona replied, 'I'll wait up.'

The trio departed to police headquarters to have a quick meeting.

The night's full moon created shadows everywhere. Street lighting was generally only on corners. They travelled to the meeting place in silence.

James wondered what was driving Kennedy. Was it payback over his capture with the Marsh kidnap debacle, or something more sinister? Would he listen to reason, just rant and rave, or even do him harm?

Richard and James drove slowly to the corner. It was almost midnight. They stopped under the corner streetlight and waited.

A voice said, 'I said no police.'

James answered. 'He is not a policeman; he is a cab driver. You did say the woman was injured and to bring a cab. Now where is the woman?'

Sean stepped forward into the lamplight holding a woman's arm. She was limping and leaning on him.

Cautiously James went to her and took her other arm and helped her to the cab.

Sean looked at Richard. 'Stay where you are. He doesn't need your help.'

As James was assisting the injured woman up to the gig step, she stumbled backward forcing James to move back as well. Up to this stage Sean had his revolver in his right hand and pressed into James's back. When James moved backwards Sean instinctively moved to the right and removed the revolver from James's back and lowered his right arm. He used his left hand to push James forward. The woman's body momentarily hid Richard from Sean's view.

Richard quickly drew his revolver. When Sean re-appeared, he saw the revolver pointed at him.

Richard called, 'I will shoot.'

Sean laughed. 'No, you won't,' and began to raise his right arm with the revolver. Richard fired twice; the two bullets hit Sean in the chest. He was killed instantly and fell to the ground.

Inspector Dodson and his constables arrived within seconds. They were behind a nearby door. He quickly took charge, ordering his men to take Sean's body to the morgue and he volunteered to take Miss Millingan to the hospital. She had a badly strained ankle and was suffering shock, but was otherwise uninjured. After dropping her at the hospital he returned to his office to write a preliminary report.

James climbed into their cab and sat down. They sat in the gig for a short time saying nothing.

Richard spoke first. 'Strange. I thought I would be nervous, but my army training came to the fore and I was very calm. As you saw my aim was good.'

James nodded. 'I don't think he was going to cause me harm. It might have been to prove a point that he had control over me, being a figure of authority. We will probably never now. Let's go. The paperwork can wait.' He waved goodnight to the inspector and left the crime scene.

Richard dropped James back at the *Carlisle*. The foyer light was still on, as was the one in a small ante room. A doorman ushered him into the ante room and served him tea and hot scones. It was only then he realised how hungry he was. The doorman said Fiona requested she be woken when he returned. James told him to let her sleep; he would see her in the morning. He was shown to his bedroom where he fell into a deep sleep.

Following a discreet knock on his door, a doorman entered carrying a change of clothes. 'I trust these are your size. I had a guess.' They were. James was advised lunch would be served at noon and it was now eleven a.m.

After a wash, he dressed in his new clothes, and walked to the dining room. He was pleased to see Fiona.

She asked, 'How are you? I was worried about you. What time did you get in? I waited up.'

He replied, 'I think around four a.m. I let you sleep. I was mentally and physically exhausted and besides I knew I'd meet you today.' He kissed her.

Her parents arrived and they had a pleasant lunch. Arthur Giles asked James if he could talk about what happened last night. He presumed it was urgent police business.

At that moment Inspector Dodson arrived requesting a meeting with James.

Arthur said, 'Let's adjourn to the sunroom.'

Inspector Dodson had completed a report on the evening's events and wanted James's opinion on its accuracy.

He looked towards Arthur who nodded. Inspector Dodson read the report, it took five minutes. They listened in silence.

James agreed with the report but said he and Richard would add a page or two on Monday.

Arthur shook his head. 'Well, you lead an exciting life, young man.'

Fiona sat there just looking at James thinking, *I've already lost a loved one. I hope I don't lose another one.*

The meeting ended.

Fiona took James's arm and they walked into the garden.

James asked, 'I saw the inspector look to your father before he started speaking and he allowed him to listen to his report. You said he was in the public service. Just what does your father do?'

Fiona laughed. 'My father is Sir Arthur William Giles KBE – Knight of the British Empire. He is a public servant and the Victorian Government Treasurer. I thought you knew.'

James said, 'I owe your father an apology; right now. He is over there. Let me speak with him alone please.'

He waved to Sir Arthur to attract his attention. 'Sir, may I speak with you?'

Sir Arthur nodded. 'I was hoping we could have a chat by ourselves.'

James spoke first. 'I was unaware of your position in the community. I owe you an apology for not showing you due deference.'

Sir Arthur laughed. 'I had presumed that. It is not a problem. While we're by ourselves, I gather you and Fiona are very fond of each other and your relationship is serious. She is our only daughter, so I watch out for her. She is well educated, presentable and is a shareholder in the family Cumberland Estate Company.'

James replied, 'Yes, Fiona invited me there. It's an excellent property.' He hesitated. 'I intend to ask her to marry me. Can I have your permission? I realise you do not know me very well, but I do love her, and I have a career and I own a fifty per cent share in a property near Cumberland Estate. I can support her adequately.'

Sir Giles did not answer immediately. They kept walking.

He eventually spoke. 'Her mother was impressed with you and, frankly, we had asked around about you, so we do know of your background and current situation. Yes, we believe you are an honourable man. You have our permission.' They shook hands.

James walked back to Fiona and sat beside her.

She asked, 'Are you forgiven?' He didn't need to reply.

He just said, 'I asked your father for permission to marry you.'

She stared at him. 'Shouldn't you ask me first?'

'I took advantage of the opportunity. Will you marry me?'

Fiona shouted. 'Yes. Yes. Yes,' and hugged him. Arm in arm they went to tell her parents.

James had to return to the courthouse to prepare for the next day's hearings. He was very impressed by the *Carlisle* and suggested that this would be a perfect place to have their wedding reception.

Fiona said, 'Yes, that won't be a problem.'

James asked, 'Why? Do you know someone?'

She laughed. 'Yes, this is owned by the Cumberland Estate Company and I'm a shareholder. My parents live upstairs above the reception area.'

James was at a loss for words. What other surprises did Fiona have for in store for him?

The following week, he and Alan made the captain an offer of two hundred pounds for his property. He accepted and vacated within two days. Joseph moved into their new farm, christened *Little Woodlea* by Mavis. The next day James hired a local tradesman to completely repaint Joseph's former cottage, both inside and out and upgraded the furniture. Joseph had erected a homemade shower in the laundry. It was a four-gallon drum mounted in the ceiling with a garden watering can spout in its base and a tap that was operated by a hand lever. The drum was filled by a hand pump from an outside water tank. It was now a gentleman farmer's weekender.

With the purchase of a new property, together with James and Fiona's engagement, the four decided to have a weekend at *Woodlea*. They hired a chef to prepare and serve a banquet dinner for them and to save any of them having to cook, particularly the women.

James and Fiona arrived mid-afternoon from Melbourne. Fiona was shown to the guest room in the main house. The four of them walked down to the river where Alan demonstrated his skill at trout tickling, unfortunately without success. They then shared a bottle of expensive vintage wine, some nibbles and they all toasted their good fortune.

Alan said, 'Who would have thought James's attempted kidnapping would have brought us to this. A company with two fully owned properties worth around five hundred pounds in less than three years. Ironically, if it was not for Sean Kennedy, we would not have met or have been standing in front of the courthouse when we met Fiona. Is 'met' that the right word?' They all laughed and toasted Sean Kennedy.

The decision Alan and James had made, to find a new lifestyle in a new country, had been successful. The two were now notable local personalities in their own right, in a new and exciting land with enormous potential and future.

Their banquet dinner that night would be remembered for many years. The food was excellent, as was the service.

After dinner Alan and Mavis retired to bed and James and Fiona went for a walk. The wedding was to be in three weeks, and they needed to decide where their home was to be. They eventually decided to call *Cumberland Estate* their main home and occasionally stay at *Woodlea* in the cottage or with her parents at *Carlisle* in Melbourne. He would keep his courthouse room. James kissed her and left Fiona at the main house.

She said, 'I'll be over for a shower in the morning. Leave your door unlocked.'

James was still asleep when Fiona entered the cottage for her shower. James had warned her the water would be cold and smiled to himself when he heard her gasp as the cold water poured over her. He was lying in bed still half asleep when he sensed her presence. He looked up and saw Fiona drop her towel and reveal a beautiful naked woman who then climb into his bed. For a second or so he saw her two magnificent bouncing breasts and the next moment felt them against him.

She said, 'Mavis and Alan have gone to town. We're on our own.' Fiona began kissing him, gently moving her lips on his.

James started to respond to her, when he suddenly remembered her father's praise of him – *You are an honourable man.* He stopped kissing and looked at her. He had his hand on her breast and she had her hand on him. He thought – *Could I be honourable? Yes. Should I be honourable? Yes. Would I be honourable?* He would soon know!

ADDENDUM

1   Extracts from an 1886 Shearing Contract
2   Shearing Union and Australian Workers' Union
3   *The Shearers* by Henry Lawson
4   Agriculture college – Late 1800's
5   Wages – 1860

Addendum 1   EXTRACTS FROM AN 1886 SHEARING CONTRACT

SPECIFICATIONS OF SHEARING CONTRACTS

All sheep to be carried from the pen and put quietly down on the floor.

The crutch, brisket and points to be properly trimmed and the belly wool to be removed injuring the fleece by twice-cutting.

In opening the fleece at the neck, both blades of the shears to be kept under the wool and close to the skin so as to prevent twice-cutting. No shearer allowed to run his shearers through the fleece so as to break it down the centre or back.

No shearer allowed to put his foot or knee on any sheep.

Any shearer injuring any sheep or cutting any of the teats of any ewe or lamb or ram will forfeit 8 shillings.

Any shearer turning out a sheep with a cut insufficiently tarred shall at once bring it back to the shearing floor and tar the wound.

All sheep with horns growing into the head or eyes and any unmarked lambs, to be put back to the catching pen by the shearer or forfeit price for sheep.

Rules

1. Shearers will be paid at the rate of 17 shillings and sixpence per hundred sheep.
2. Working hours from 6am to 6pm, except on Saturdays, when shearing will cease at 4 pm generally.
3. One smoko of 15 minutes will be allowed in the morning and two similar in the afternoon.
4. No shearer to catch sheep while his pen is being filled.
5. No swearing, bad language or disorderly conduct allowed in the shed and no talking during working hours.
6. Any shearer who is discharged through misconduct or bad shearing will be paid at the rate of 10 shillings per hundred and will be charged at the rate of 14 shillings per week for his board.
7. Any person engaged as a shearer who is afterwards found not to be a shearer shall forfeit whatever money may be due to him and to be prosecuted for breach of contract.
8. Any shearer bringing intoxicating liquor onto the station shall be liable to a fine of 20s and also to instant dismissal.
9. No grog shall be brought to the shed or huts thereof.
10. No shearer allowed to shear more than 100 sheep in any per day.

SIGNED: GEORGE WALES

Addendum 2   THE AUSTRALIAN WORKERS' UNION

At a Conference of the Amalgamated Shearers' Union of Australasia and the General Labourers Union of Australasia held in Sydney, February 1894, it was decided that both Unions should amalgamate under the name of the Australian Workers' Union. The following General Rules were the outcome of the work of the Revising Committee and formed the Rules governing the A.W.U. pending the completion at an Intercolonial Convention to be held in February 1895.

RULES OF THE AUSTRALIAN WORKERS' UNION

1. The name of this Society shall be the "Australian Workers' Union" and it shall consist of as many branches and sections as may conform to the following rules:

OBJECTS

2. The objects of the Union shall be as follows:

   (a) To defend the rights of the workers by combining together for mutual aid and protection.
   (b) To secure and maintain a fair rate of remuneration for shearing and other classes of labour.
   (c) To secure the adoption and enforcement of just and equitable agreements between employers and employees.

(d) To protect members against exorbitant charges for rations, requisites or accommodation.

(e) To provide legal assistance in defence of members' rights.

(f) To improve the relations between employers and employees and to settle disputes by means of conciliation and arbitration.

(g) To establish a fund for relief of members in case of accident.

(h) To provide employment for members and other Unionists by establishing co-operative enterprises and works of various kinds.

(i) To secure such political reform as will give justice to the workers by assisting to return men to Parliament pledged to legislate in that direction.

(j) To establish and maintain Labour journals.

(k) To assist kindred organisations in upholding the rights and privileges of workers and generally to assist in the emancipation of Labour.

(l) To provide funds for the accomplishment of these objects by contributions, levies, fines, donations, etc., from members and others.

Addendum 3   THE SHEARERS
Henry Lawson 1895

No church bell rings them from the Track,
No pulpit lights their blindness–
'Tis hardship, drought, and homelessness
That teach those Bushmen kindness:
The mateship born, in barren lands,
Of toil and thirst and danger,
The camp-fare for the wanderer set,
The first place to the stranger.

They do the best they can today–
Take no thought of the morrow;
Their way is not the old-world way–
They live to lend and borrow.
When shearing's done and cheques gone wrong,
They call in "time to slither!"–
They saddle up and say "So-long!"
And ride – the Lord knows whither.

And though he may be brown or black,
Or wrong man there, or right man,
The mate that's steadfast to his mates
They call that man a "white man!"
They tramp in mateship side by side–
The Protestant and the Roman–
They call no biped lord or sir,
And touch their hat to no man!

They carry in their swags, perhaps,
A portrait and a letter–
And, maybe, deep down in their hearts,
The hope of "something better."
Where lonely miles are hard to ride,
And long, hot days recurrent,
There's lots of time to think of men
They might have been–but weren't.

They turn their faces to the west
And leave the world behind them
(Their drought-dry graves are seldom set
Where even mates can find them).
They know too little of the world
To rise to wealth and greatness;
But in these lines I'll gladly pay
My tribute to their greatness.

Addendum 4   AGRICULTURE COLLEGES

During the late 1800's, the colonies established Agriculture Colleges in their major cities. The diploma course of instruction was for two years. The first year's subjects were:

a. Practical agriculture
b. Principles of Agriculture
c. Practical chemistry
d. Theoretical chemistry
e. Botany (including vegetable pathology)
f. Arithmetic
g. English
h. Surveying

The second year's subjects added:

a. Entomology
b. Veterinary science
c. Bookkeeping
d. Applied mechanics and heat
e. Sheep and wool

Students entering for practical work of a farm were expected to be able to perform any of the following:

Milk cows, kill and dress sheep, detailed carpentering work, blacksmithing, fencing, bullocking, orchard work, handle horses for sowing and reaping work, handling general farm implements, operating mechanical machinery, and answer questions on:

Soil suitability or crops, cultivation and harvesting, fallow land and green manuring, manuring of crops, costings of implements, value of irrigation and drainage, farm layout including buildings and fences, value of silos and silage, vegetable gardens, vineyards, and orchards, livestock care and business management.

Many immigrants to the colonies had been farmers and some became squatters occupying large land holdings. They started Australia's sheep, cattle and grain industry helped by the shearers, the fencers, the stockmen and the many other itinerant bush men. The introduction of the Agriculture Colleges Degree Graduates, further progressed Australia's position in the world as a major primary producer.

Addendum 5   WAGES – 1860

Mechanics and labourers – Per day

Carpenter	9s to 11 shillings
Masons	9s to 11s
Brick setters	13s to 14s
Plasterers	10s to 12s
Painters	9s to 10s
Printers	10s to 13s
Boilermakers	12/6
Smiths	11/6
Engineers	11/6
Labourers	7-9s
Coppersmiths	9/6
Iron founders	9-13s

Domestic servants – Per annum

Male servants	30 to 46 Pounds
Cooks	20 to 60 Pounds
Gardeners	35 to 45 Pounds
Laundresses	26 to 30 Pounds
Grooms	40 to 50 Pounds
Female servants	20 to 26 Pounds
Nursemaids	20 to 25 Pounds
Housemaids	20 to 26 Pounds

Country workers – Per annum plus rations

Farm labourers	30 to 40 Pounds
Shepherds	25 to 30 Pounds
Married couples	40 to 50 Pounds
Stockman	40 to 50 Pounds
Hut keepers	20 to 25 Pounds
Bullock drivers	40 to 50 Pounds

Rations - Per week

Flour	8 to 12 lbs.
Meat	10 to 12 lbs.
Sugar	2 lbs.
Tea	¼ lb.

AUTHOR

John P F Lynch has written several history, historical fiction books and a biography. Most books are in the Australian National Archives and in state libraries. The focus has been on colonial history in the 1850-1870 era, interrelated with an entertaining storyline.

He has travelled extensively during his sixty-year career in aviation and has visited County Clare in Ireland and Cumbria in Northern England several times to research his books.

John is a member of the Order of Australia, a Knight Hospitaller of the Order of St John of Jerusalem and a Fellow of the Royal Victorian Association of Honorary Justices.

He is an ex-navy veteran and was the president of the Romsey/Lancefield RSL just on ten years. He is also a former president and secretary of the Romsey Football/Netball Club and a Life Member of both. He is a reserve member of the Macedon Ranges Legacy Group having served as a chairman of the group, board member of the Bendigo Club and long-standing Sergeant of Arms. His current main community involvement is as vice president of the Craigieburn War Memorial Remembrance Committee.

He is now retired and lives with his wife in the Craigieburn Retirement Village in Victoria.

OTHER BOOKS by J. P. F. Lynch

The Convict and the Soldier
The Aborigine and the Drover
The Constable and the Miner
A Challenging Decade – 1940'S

LOCAL HISTORY

History of the Romsey Football/Netball Club 1878-2009
History of St Mary's Parish 1858-2006
History of the Romsey/Lancefield RSL 1933-2008
Joseph Hall - Kyneton pioneer 1804-1872

AUTOBIOGRAPHY

A Lifetime's Journey

www.ingramcontent.com/pod-product-compliance
Lightning Source LLC
Chambersburg PA
CBHW070546010526
44118CB00012B/1243